QUICKBOOKS U
in easy step

CW00739754

Stephen Copestake

COMPUTER
STEP

In easy steps is an imprint of Computer Step
Southfield Road . Southam
Warwickshire CV33 OFB . England

Tel: 01926 817999 Fax: 01926 817005
http://www.computerstep.com

Printed and bound in the United Kingdom

ISBN 1-874029-83-0

Contents

First steps

This chapter shows you how to get started quickly in QuickBooks UK. You'll learn to open/close it, familiarise yourself with the screen, and use the Navigator. You'll also discover how to back up/restore data, and you'll learn how to get information from the on-line Help system (including Inside Tips, Qcards and QuickTour). Finally (if you have a viable Internet connection) you'll connect to the QuickBooks World Wide Web site, for help which is even more topical.

Chapter One

Covers

Starting/closing QuickBooks

Launching QuickBooks

To run QuickBooks UK, click the Start button in the bottom left-hand corner of the Windows screen:

You can create a shortcut to launch QuickBooks directly. See your Windows documentation for how to do this.

(If the Start button isn't currently visible, move the mouse pointer over the bottom of the screen to make the Windows Task bar appear, *then* click the Start button.)

Now do the following:

Click here

3 Click here

Start button

2 Click here

You can use a useful keyboard shortcut to close QuickBooks. Simply press Alt+F4.

Closing QuickBooks

Refer to the upper right-hand corner of the QuickBooks UK screen and do the following:

Click here

The QuickBooks screen

When it starts, QuickBooks displays whatever screen components were open when you last closed it.

The illustration below shows one of many possible configurations:

Title bar   Menu bar

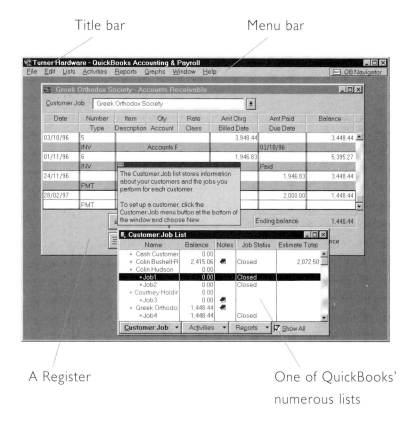

A Register   One of QuickBooks' numerous lists

The illustration also shows a Qcard:

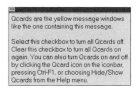

See page 22 for how to use Qcards.

The Navigator – an overview

One screen component which you'll almost certainly want to use frequently is the Navigator.

The Navigator provides the following:

- tabs which supply access to major program areas e.g.

  — Sales and Customers

  — Purchasing and Vendors

  — Company information

- icons which jump to lists

- icons which jump to activities

- access to reports

The illustration below shows the Navigator in action:

See Chapter Two for more information on QuickBooks UK companies.

Tabs   List icons

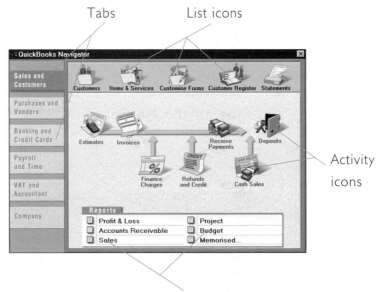

Activity icons

Available reports

Displaying/hiding the Navigator

Launching the Navigator

If QuickBooks UK doesn't automatically display the Navigator when you start it, you can easily rectify this.

Carrying out the procedure on the right when the Navigator is on-screen but currently hidden behind other windows brings it to the fore.

Do the following:

Click here

When you close the Navigator, a special message launches. Do the following:

Click here

Closing the Navigator

If you don't want to use the Navigator, do the following:

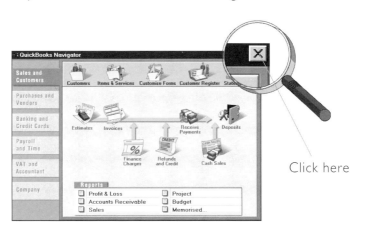

Click here

Click here

Using the Navigator

Jumping to QuickBooks areas
Do the following:

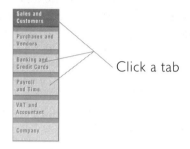

Click a tab

Jumping to QuickBooks lists
Do the following:

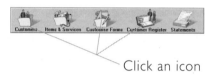

Click an icon

After carrying out any of the actions here, complete any messages or submenus which appear.

Jumping to major activities
Do the following:

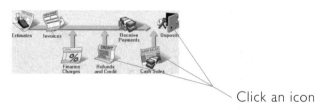

Click an icon

Viewing reports
Do the following:

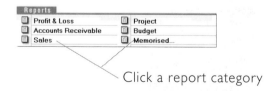

Click a report category

Backing up data

Before you can use QuickBooks UK, you need to create at least one company. (See Chapter Two for how to do this.) When you create a company, however, QuickBooks generates a specific internal file which contains all the relevant data. All QuickBooks files have the following suffix:

.QBW

Clearly, this file is of crucial importance to your business. You need to evolve a backup strategy which ensures that, in the event of data loss/corruption or hard disk failure, no data is lost. You should:

You can use the backup/ restore process as a way of transferring QuickBooks data between separate PCs.

- back up data at the end of *every* QuickBooks session

- make a separate monthly backup (and store it at a different location)

- keep several sets of appropriately labelled floppy disks (one for each day of the week) and back up to the appropriate disk every day

Fortunately, QuickBooks UK makes it easy to create backup sets.

Carrying out a backup

Pull down the File menu and do the following:

Click here

Now perform the following:

2 Name the backup file   **3** Click here

You can also back up onto another hard disk (if you have more than one installed).
   Simply select the hard disk in step 1. Select a folder here: Then follow steps 2 and 3.

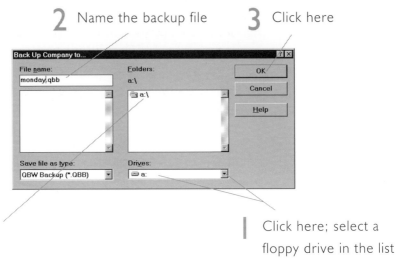

Click here; select a floppy drive in the list

QuickBooks UK now begins the backup process and displays this message:

Backup files are much smaller than the original QuickBooks data files. However, if they won't fit onto a single floppy disk, QuickBooks will spread them onto subsequent disks.
   Simply follow the on-screen instructions.

When QuickBooks has finished the backup, a further message appears. Do the following:

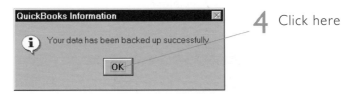

4 Click here

Restoring data

In the event of data loss, insert the latest backup disk into your floppy drive. (If your backup extends over more than one disk, insert the first.) Then do the following:

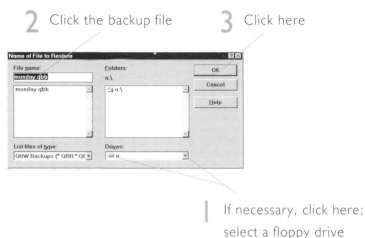

2 Click the backup file

3 Click here

 Backup files must be *restored* onto your hard disk: they can't be copied and then opened in the normal way.

If necessary, click here; select a floppy drive

6 Name the restored file

7 Click here

4 Click here; select a hard drive in the list

5 Select a folder

8 Click here

Using Help

QuickBooks UK has an on-line Help system which allows you to get *context-sensitive* assistance. This is assistance which is tailored to whatever you happen to be doing at the time. For example, if you want assistance with a specific dialog, QuickBooks will provide it, and in considerable detail.

Launching Help

Pull down the Help menu and click Help. Now do any of the following:

HANDY TIP

Click any of these buttons to access additional Help features.

Left-click any related topic (underlined, and in green) for more help

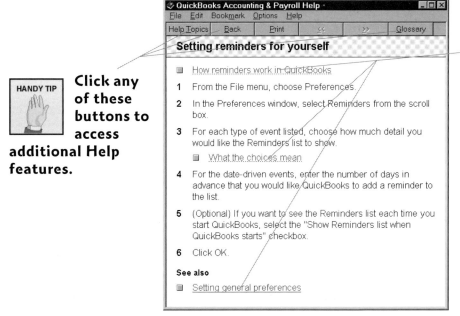

To close Help when you've finished with it, press Esc (or Alt+F4).

...contd

Any QuickBooks UK Help screen provides access to the following:

- Contents (a list of topics and sub-topics)

- Index (an alphabetical list of topics)

- Find (an indexed Help database)

Using Contents

In QuickBooks, click Help in the Help menu. Click the Help Topics button. Then carry out the following:

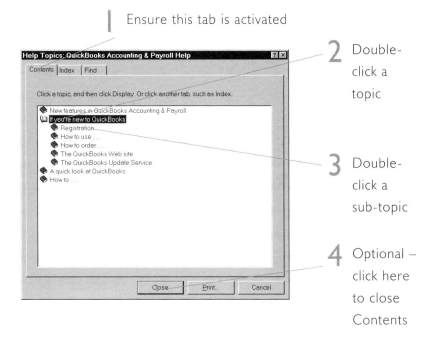

Ensure this tab is activated

2 Double-click a topic

3 Double-click a sub-topic

4 Optional – click here to close Contents

As an alternative to step 4, you can simply press the Esc key.

...contd

Using Index

In QuickBooks, click Help in the Help menu. Click the Help Topics button. Then carry out the following:

Ensure this tab is activated

To close a Help window at any time, simply press Esc.

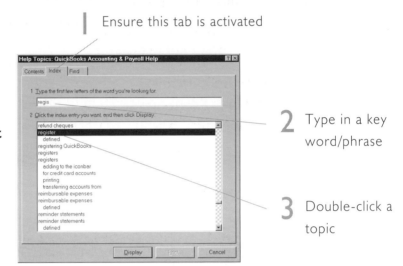

2 Type in a key word/phrase

3 Double-click a topic

Using Find

In QuickBooks, click Help in the Help menu. Click the Help Topics button. Then carry out the following:

The Find window enables you to locate instances (within the overall QuickBooks UK Help file) where the key words you enter are associated. Use Find if the other methods don't work.

Ensure this tab is activated

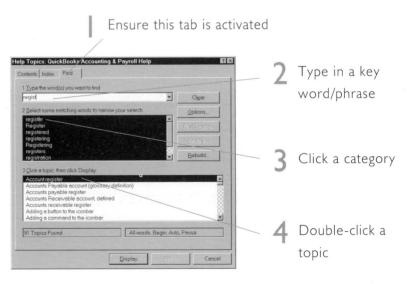

2 Type in a key word/phrase

3 Click a category

4 Double-click a topic

Using Inside Tips

QuickBooks UK has a feature which makes it even easier to find relevant assistance: Inside Tips. This is a special dialog which provides a list of hints and tips. You can:

• view a complete list of tips

• have the Quicken Tips dialog display automatically each time you run Quicken

Pull down the Help menu and click Inside Tips. Now carry out steps 1–2 below to view an alternative tip. Finally, follow step 3.

3 Click here to close
the dialog

Ensure this is selected to have the Inside Tips dialog launch automatically whenever you run QuickBooks UK.

Click here to view
the next tip

2 Double-click a
tip to view it

Using QuickTour

QuickBooks UK comes with an in-built introduction: QuickTour. QuickTour provides hands-on help with:

- program features (stressing aspects which make using QuickBooks UK easy – e.g. the compiling of customer, vendor and stock lists)

- basic concepts covering the following broad areas:

  — sales

  — accounts payable

  — stock management

  — VAT tracking

Launching QuickTour

Press Ctrl+Esc. Now do the following:

Click here

2 Click here   3 Click here

...contd

Now carry out the following:

Click here to close QuickTour when you've finished using it.

Click either of these buttons, then follow the on-screen instructions

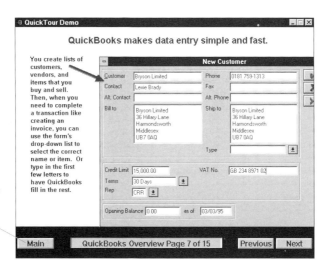

Click here to return to the main QuickTour window.

A Features window

Using Qcards

Qcards are very useful when you're new to QuickBooks UK. When you're more experienced, however, you may find they're a distraction. In this case, simply carry out step 1 to have Qcards hidden.

Qcards are a specialised Help feature. When you move the insertion point into the majority of fields in QuickBooks windows or dialogs, an explanatory box pops up with context-specific help.

Turning on the Qcards feature

Pull down the Help menu and do the following:

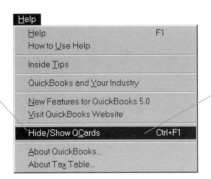

Click here

Using Qcards

Do the following:

2 Click in the appropriate field...

If you want to close a specific Qcard, simply press Esc.

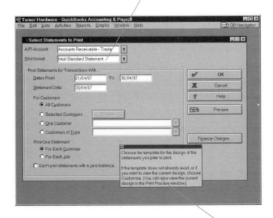

The relevant Qcard appears

Connecting to the Web site

The Web site is an on-line service which Intuit maintains in order to provide QuickBooks UK users with immediate (and extremely up-to-date) assistance. Use the Web site to:

- obtain hints/tips relating to your use of QuickBooks UK

- answer any questions you may have about your use of QuickBooks UK

- access up-to-date articles on QuickBooks UK topics. These include:

  — General information on QuickBooks UK itself

  — Accounting

  — Error messages

  — Printing

  — Reports

Requirements

To use the QuickBooks UK Web site, you must have:

- a modem connected to your PC

- an ongoing account with an Internet Service provider (e.g. AOL, Demon, MSN)

- a compatible Internet browser (for instance, Internet Explorer or Netscape Navigator – the examples shown in this section use both)

If you meet the requirements set out on page 23, there are two ways you can connect to the Web site.

Connecting directly from within QuickBooks UK

This is the quickest and most convenient method.

REMEMBER

This method of connecting to the Web site requires QuickBooks UK to be open and running at the same time.

First, ensure your PC and modem are active. Open your connection with your service provider. Now pull down the Help menu and do the following:

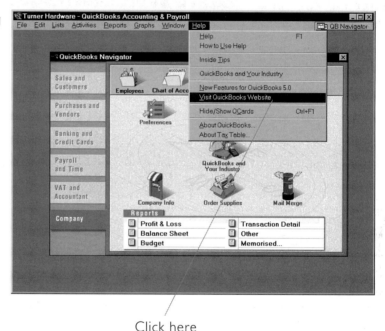

Click here

Two things now happen:

1.   your Internet browser launches

2.   a connection with QuickBooks UK's on-line World Wide Web site is automatically established, and the site is loaded into your browser

For how to use the Web site, see page 26.

...contd

Connecting from within your browser

This method is slightly more long-winded, but still convenient.

 In this method of connecting to the Web site, QuickBooks UK does not have to be open at the same time.

First, ensure your PC and modem are active. Open your connection with your service provider. Take whatever action is necessary to launch your browser. Now do the following:

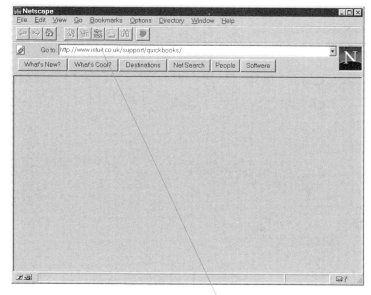

 This is Netscape Navigator. If you're using an alternative browser, follow the necessary procedure to open the Web site. (If you're using Microsoft's Internet Explorer, however, the procedure is identical.)

Type in the following:

http://www.intuit.co.uk/ support/quickbooks/

Now press Enter; your browser loads the Web site.

For how to use the Web site, see page 26.

Using the Web site

Whichever method you use to connect to the Web site, this is the result. Do either of the following:

Click any icon

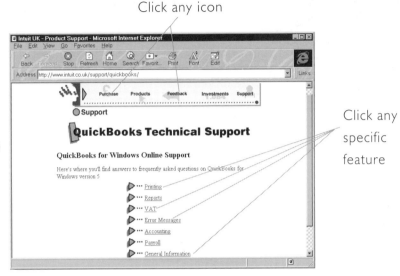

Click any specific feature

Here, the Web site's Home page is being viewed through Internet Explorer.

The next illustration shows the result of clicking on the General Information feature:

To return to the previously viewed page, press Alt+←.

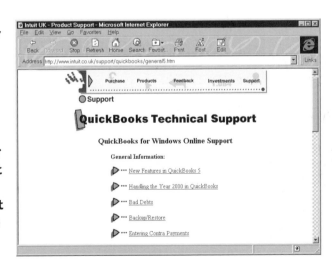

To close down your browser at any time, press Alt+F4. Don't forget to terminate your Internet connection too!

The EasyStep Interview

Creating a company based on your business is the first, essential step in your use of QuickBooks UK; this chapter shows you how to use the EasyStep Interview to do this. You'll tailor-make your use of the sections and topics in the Interview, using it as often – or as infrequently – as you want.

Covers

The Interview – an overview

Before you can do anything in QuickBooks UK, you need to create a company based on your business.

Your QuickBooks company will contain all the financial records relating to your business. If you run more than one business (and you file separate tax returns for each), you'll need to create more than one company.

There are two ways to create a company in QuickBooks:

- manually

- with the help of the EasyStep Interview

Since Intuit strongly recommends using the EasyStep Interview, this book will concentrate on that method.

The EasyStep Interview walks you through the company setup procedure. Among other things, it helps you:

- setup company details e.g.:

  — name, address and business type

  — financial/tax year details

  — whether you keep stock

- set QuickBooks operating preferences

- specify whether you want VAT tracking to be in force, and if so on what basis

- enter your company start date

- create new income and expense accounts

- set up items for products/services you provide, or for stock

- specify opening balances relating to customers, vendors and accounts

- customise two essential QuickBooks menus

...contd

 You don't have to complete the EasyStep Interview in one go. Instead, you can leave it when you want to by clicking this button:

When you restart the Interview, you return to where you left off last time.

 You should, however, bear in mind that, when you set your start date in the Start Date topic within the General section, it *is* a very good idea to get it right first time.

Interview tabs

The EasyStep Interview organises its features under the following:

- vertical tabs

- horizontal tabs

The vertical tabs relate to overall program *sections*, the horizontal tabs to *topics* within these. For example, the General (vertical) section – arguably the most important – has the following horizontal tabs (topics) associated with it:

- Welcome

- Company

- Preferences

- VAT

- Start Date

The idea is that you start at the first screen of the first topic in the first section, and work your way through subsequent windows to the next topic. Once the last topic has been completed, you move on to the next section and begin again. (However, see the Remember tip on the left if you favour a less linear approach.)

Some Interview windows require no input from the user (except an instruction to proceed to the next), while in others you make choices which affect your subsequent use of QuickBooks UK. However, none of these are irreversible: you can always change the settings you've implemented later.

Starting the Interview

Pull down the File menu and do the following:

Click here

If you're using the Interview to create *additional* **companies, the launch process is different.**

Pull down the File menu and click New Company. Now complete the (shortened) Interview.

Now do the following:

3 Ensure this is selected

2 Ensure this is selected

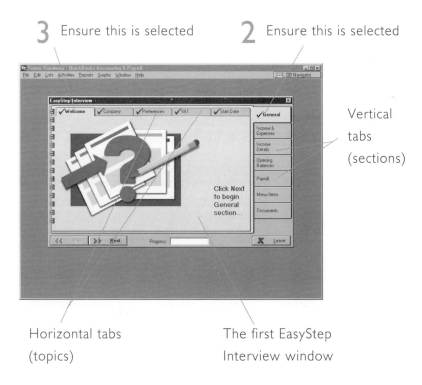

Vertical tabs (sections)

Horizontal tabs (topics)

The first EasyStep Interview window

The General tab (1)

Carry out the following steps:

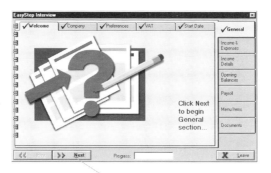

HANDY TIP

Re step 2 – if you've previously used Quicken or an earlier version of QuickBooks, and want to convert your existing file, select one of these instead:
Now follow step 3. After this, several windows launch which are specific to the conversion process. Complete these as necessary, then return to the Interview.

Click here

2 If you're not upgrading, ensure this is selected

3 Click here

HANDY TIP

Working through the General section is mandatory.

4 Click here

The General tab (2)

Two further windows now appear. As these require no input, simply click this button in each:

Now do the following:

Click here

This completes the Welcome topic. Now carry out step 2 below to begin the Company topic:

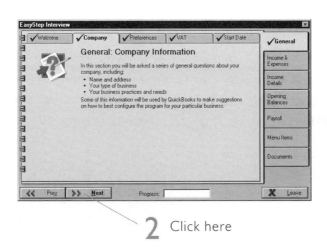

2 Click here

The General tab (3)

The Company topic is a very important one. Here, you specify settings which relate intimately to the way you'll use QuickBooks UK. Carry out the following:

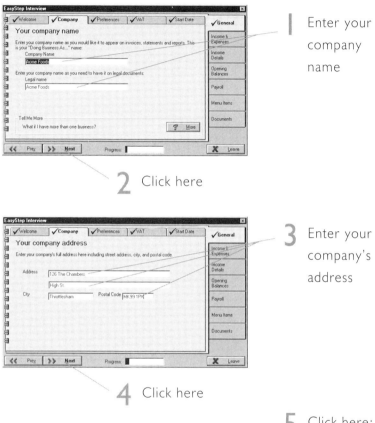

1 Enter your company name

2 Click here

3 Enter your company's address

4 Click here

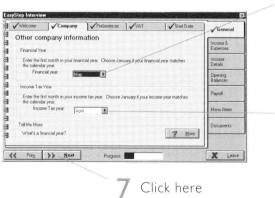

REMEMBER

Re step 5 – for many companies, the correct start month for the financial year will be January.

5 Click here; select a start month for the financial year

6 Click here; select a start month for the income tax year

7 Click here

The General tab (4)

Carry out the following steps:

If you don't perform step 1, step 2 is followed by a special message. Do the following:

Click here

Now carry out step 3 etc.

I If you're self-employed, click here; in the list, select *Self Assessment Tax Return*

2 Click here

3 Select an overall business type

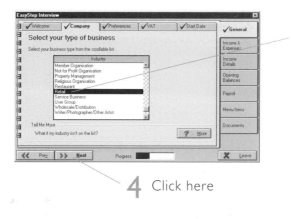

4 Click here

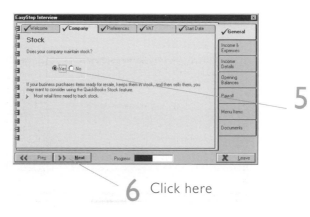

5 Click here if your company keeps stock

6 Click here

The General tab (5)

There are pros and cons to using QuickBooks UK to track stock.

For instance, if you *manufacture* products, you shouldn't track stock in QuickBooks (because it can't track finished goods). And even non-manufacturers are subject to a functional limit in terms of the number of items tracked (if you have more than around 5,000 parts, entering them into QuickBooks is unacceptably tedious).

Read the Help file for more information.

In the next window, you have the chance to view an on-line QuickBooks Help file which can help you decide whether to use QuickBooks to track stock. If you want to view the Help file, click this button:

Show Help

Scroll through the Help file. When you've finished with it, press Esc. If you didn't view the Help file, click the Next button in the Interview window.

In the subsequent window, click Yes to track stock, or No if you don't want to use this feature. Click Next. Click Next in the succeeding window. Now do the following:

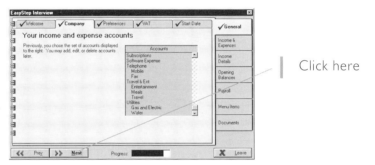

Click here

In the above, QuickBooks shows you which accounts are in your Chart of Accounts. You can alter these later, although many users don't find this necessary.

Carry out the following to complete the Company topic:

Click here

The General tab (6)

In the next window which launches, do the following:

You use the Preferences topic to:

- **determine how QuickBooks operates**
- **customise how QuickBooks looks**

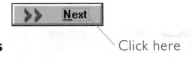

Click here

Now carry out the following steps:

1 Select an invoice format (you can change this later)

2 Click here

Re step 3 – regard anyone as an employee if you:

- **pay them**
- **remove tax at source and submit it to the Inland Revenue QuickBooks UK does not regard sub-contractors as employees.**

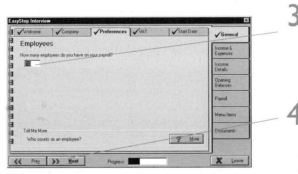

3 Type in the number of staff you employ

4 Click here

In the next three windows, do the following:

Time tracking is beyond the scope of this book.

- click Yes if you send out estimates, then click Next

- click Yes if you prepare *partial* invoices, then click Next

- click Yes if you want to use time tracking, then click Next

The General tab (7)

Classes are categories which you can apply to QuickBooks UK transactions to differentiate them.

For instance, companies with more than one department can apply separate classes to each. In this way, income and expenses can be monitored very accurately.

Users of Quicken will already be familiar with categories/classes.

In the next window, you can opt to use QuickBooks UK classes. Do the following:

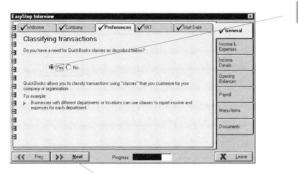

| Optional – click here to activate the classes feature

2 Click here

In the next window, you tell QuickBooks how to handle bills and payments.

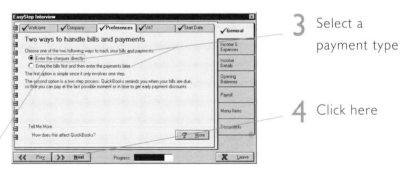

3 Select a payment type

4 Click here

Re step 3 – for the sake of clarity, this book assumes you pay your bills in one go. If you don't, select this option now. Then complete the additional windows (relating to vendor lists) which appear later in the Interview.

In the next window, you tell QuickBooks when you want its Reminders list (details of outstanding transactions) to appear. The default is each time you start QuickBooks; Intuit recommends retaining this. If you want a different basis, however, select one of the following:

- When I ask for it

- Rarely

Either way, click the Next button to proceed.

The General tab (8)

Re step 2 – if your company isn't VAT-registered (e.g. because its turnover is below the threshold – currently around £47,000 p.a. – or because it's exempt), click No instead.

If you follow this option, after step 3 the Interview jumps straight to the Start Date topic – see page 40.

The next window completes the Preferences topic; click Next to move on to the VAT topic. Then carry out the following:

I Click here

2 Click here if you want to track VAT

3 Click here

Re step 4 – if you need help completing the flagged sections, consult your local HM Customs and Excise office.

Click Next in the subsequent window (which requires no user input). Now perform the following:

4 Complete these sections

5 Click here

The General tab (9)

HANDY TIP

Re step 1 – most businesses use the Accrual report method, which results in VAT being allocated *before* payments are made. If this is the case, click:
Report VAT on an accrual basis

However, if you've arranged a Cash Accounting report basis with HM Customs and Excise (e.g. if you often receive overdue payments), click:
Report VAT on a cash basis

In the next window, you specify which VAT payment method you use. Do the following:

1 Select a payment method

2 Click here

3 Select an entry type

4 Click here

REMEMBER

Re step 3 – choose Net to enter invoices and cash sales exclusive of VAT, or Gross to enter them inclusive of VAT.
If you sell products/services to the public, you should select Gross.

Now carry out step 5 below to complete the VAT topic:

5 Click here

The General tab (10)

Changing your start date later is a difficult and time-consuming process. Therefore, you should ensure that you select a suitable date now.

The final topic in the General section now launches. The Start Date topic is an important one. You use this to set the date from which your QuickBooks accounts begin.

When you select your start date, you should bear the following in mind:

- Intuit recommends using the end of your previous financial year. This is particularly applicable if you've just started your *current* financial year

- The more recent the start date, the fewer transactions you'll have to enter later

Before you allocate your start date, make sure you have the following to hand:
- **all relevant account balances (e.g. asset and liability)**
- **all transactions entered in the period from the start date to the current date**
- **all bank or credit card transactions which hadn't been cleared at the start date**
- **all relevant statements (e.g. bank, savings and credit cards)**

- The later the start date, the more detail you can generate in QuickBooks reports

Entering your start date

Click the Next button in the first two Start Date windows. Then do the following:

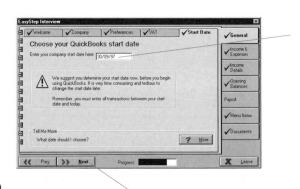

Enter your start date

2 Click here

Click the Next button in the subsequent window; this completes the General section.

The Income & Expenses tab (1)

Income and expense accounts are a useful way to keep track of income and expenses, respectively.

In the Income & Expenses topic, QuickBooks UK:

- displays the current income and expense accounts which it has set up as part of the Interview

- lets you add new income and expense accounts

In the first window, click the Next button. Now do the following:

Existing income accounts

Click here if you want to add one or more new income accounts

Re step 1 – if you select No, skip steps 3 and 4.

2 Click here

Unlike many other programs, QuickBooks UK does not number accounts.

3 Name the new account here

After you've added accounts here, you can rename or delete them later – see Chapter Three.
   You can also add new accounts.

4 Click here

In the window after step 4, click Yes to add another new income account (then click Next, and carry out steps 3 and 4 above). Alternatively, click No, then click Next.

In the final window in the Income Accts topic, click Next.

The Income & Expenses tab (2)

We're now in the Expense Accts topic. In the first window, click *one* of the following:

- More Details (to have QuickBooks UK provide brief notes on the use of expense accounts and subaccounts)

- No Thank You (to skip the explanation)

Now click the Next button. If you selected the More Details option, read the two subsequent windows and click Next in each. If you selected No Thank You, on the other hand, you jump straight to this window:

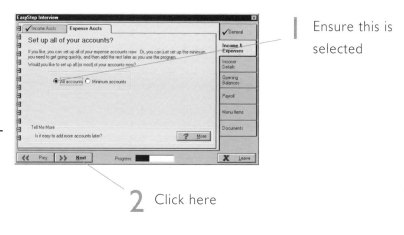

Ensure this is selected

HANDY TIP **Re step 3 – if you select No, skip steps 1 and 2 on page 43.**

2 Click here

Existing expense accounts

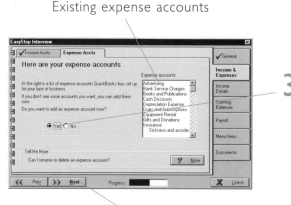

HANDY TIP **After you've added accounts here, you can rename or delete them later – see Chapter Three. You can also add new accounts.**

3 Click here if you want to add one or more new expense accounts

4 Click here

The Income & Expenses tab (3)

Now carry out the following steps:

HANDY TIP

To allocate a subaccount to an account, first follow step 1 to name it. Click here: Now click here: In the list, select the account you want the subaccount associated with. Finally, carry out step 2.

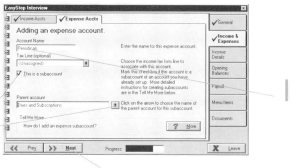

| Name the new account here

2 Click here

REMEMBER

Every business transaction and every change in the value of your business are categorised as an account. Your Chart of Accounts is simply a list of all the detailed categories your business uses.

Note: subaccounts

It's sometimes useful to set up 'child' accounts (QuickBooks UK calls these 'subaccounts') under an overall 'parent' account. For instance, QuickBooks automatically includes a parent account called Dues and Subscriptions in your Chart of Accounts. If it's helpful to you to itemise Dues and Subscriptions expenditure in greater detail, you could set up a subaccount called 'Periodicals'.

See the Handy Tip on the left for how to set up subaccounts.

In the window after step 2 above, click Yes to add another new expense account (then click Next, and carry out steps 1 and 2 above). Alternatively, click No, then click Next.

In the final window in the Expense Accts topic, click Next. This completes the Income & Expenses section.

The Income Details tab (1)

In the Income Details section, you give QuickBooks UK the following information:

The answers you enter in the Income Details section determine which parts of the QuickBooks accounts receivable facility are installed. (Accounts receivable is the accounting term for money owed to you but not yet paid.)

The Introduction topic	details of whether or not you receive full and immediate payment for the goods or services you provide
The Items topic	details of income items
The Stock topic	stock details (if applicable)

In the first window in the Introduction topic, click the Next button. Now do the following:

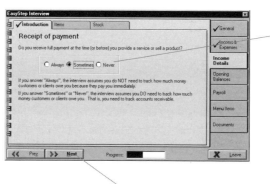

Select a payment option

Click here

Re step 1 – most businesses should find the Sometimes option most suitable (i.e. sometimes payment is received before or at the time of an order, and sometimes – or more often – it isn't).

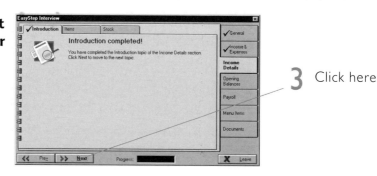

Click here

This completes the Introduction topic.

The Income Details tab (2)

Carry out the following steps:

REMEMBER

Items are an integral part of using QuickBooks UK. You allocate an item for every product or service you provide; QuickBooks tracks them for you and provides sales reports (details of how they're moving) on demand. Items appear on QuickBooks forms and invoices.

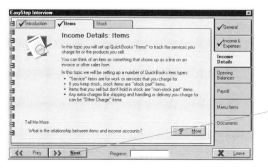

1 Click here

2 Click here if you want to add one or more items for services

3 Click here

HANDY TIP

Re step 2 – if you select No instead, skip steps 4–8.

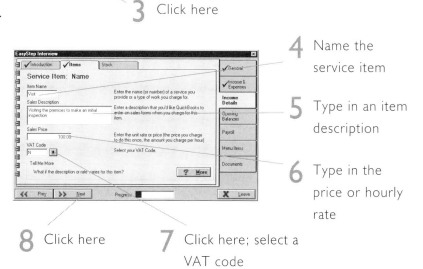

4 Name the service item

5 Type in an item description

6 Type in the price or hourly rate

8 Click here

7 Click here; select a VAT code

The Income Details tab (3)

In the next window, you tell QuickBooks UK which income account you want the new item associated with.

HANDY TIP

Re step 1 – if none of the existing income accounts is suitable, you can create a new one on-the-fly.

Choose <Add New> in the list. The New Account dialog launches; complete this, then click OK. Finally, follow step 2.

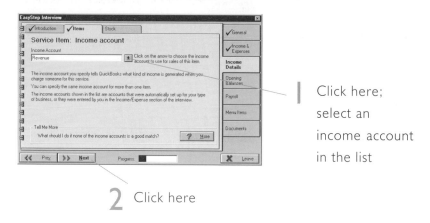

Click here; select an income account in the list

2 Click here

Carry out step 3 below if you don't use subcontractors to perform the service represented by the item (however, see the Remember tip on the left if you do), then follow step 4:

REMEMBER

Re step 3 – if you do make use of subcontractors, click Yes instead. Perform step 4. Complete the next two windows which launch, clicking Next in each when you've finished. Finally, jump to steps 1 and 2 on page 47.

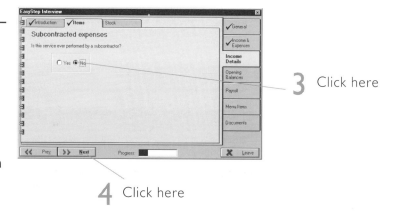

3 Click here

4 Click here

The Income Details tab (4)

Re step 1 – if you want to create further service items, click Yes instead. Now follow the appropriate steps on pages 45 and 46.
Repeat this procedure as often as necessary. When you've created enough service items, follow steps 1–2 on the right.

Now carry out the following steps:

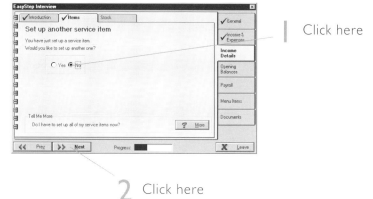

1 Click here

2 Click here

QuickBooks UK makes a distinction between:

You can easily create further service items *outside* the Interview.

Stock part items	items which you purchase, keep in stock for a time and then sell on
Non-stock part items	items which you purchase and sell on immediately, or which are sold without having been bought in the first place

Follow step 3 below to create one or more non-stock part items, then step 4. If you *don't* want to create non-stock part items, select No in step 3, then follow step 4 (and omit steps 1–7 on page 48, and 1–4 on page 49).

Some businesses are happy to work with non-stock part items exclusively. The disadvantage, however, is that QuickBooks tracks less information: only details of how much has been spent or taken.

3 Click here

4 Click here

The Income Details tab (5)

Now do the following:

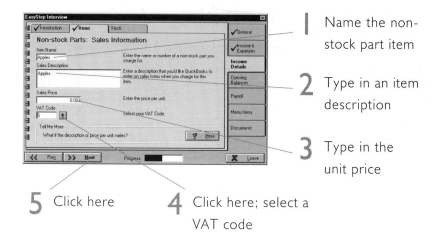

1 Name the non-stock part item

2 Type in an item description

3 Type in the unit price

5 Click here

4 Click here; select a VAT code

In the next window, you tell QuickBooks UK which income account you want the new item to be associated with.

Carry out the following steps:

HANDY TIP

Re step 6 – if none of the existing income accounts is suitable, you can create a new one on-the-fly.

Choose <Add New> in the list. The New Account dialog launches; complete this, then click OK. Finally, follow step 7.

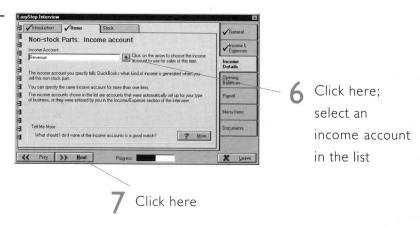

6 Click here; select an income account in the list

7 Click here

The Income Details tab (6)

**Re step 1 –
if you do
buy the
item from
a customer, click
Yes instead.
Perform step 2.
Complete the next
two windows which
launch, clicking
Next in each when
you've finished.
Finally, carry out
steps 3–4 below.**

Carry out step 1 below if you don't buy the non-stock part item from a specific customer (however, see the Remember tip on the left if you do), then carry out step 2:

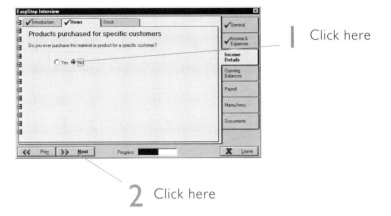

1 Click here

2 Click here

Now perform steps 3–4 below (but see the Handy Tip if you want to create additional non-stock part items at this stage):

**Re step 3 –
if you want
to create
further
non-stock part
items, click Yes
instead. Now follow
the appropriate
steps on pages 47
and 48 (and 1–2
above).
Repeat this
procedure as often
as necessary. When
you've created
enough non-stock
part items, follow
steps 3–4 on the
right.**

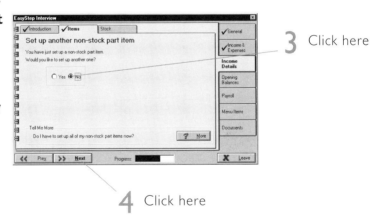

3 Click here

4 Click here

The Income Details tab (7)

REMEMBER

Re step 1 – if you do need to set up an Other Charges item, click Yes. Perform step 2. Complete the next two windows which launch, clicking Next in each when you've finished. If the item is one for which you are reimbursed by your customer, click Yes in the third window (then complete the next two); if not, click No followed by Next.

Finally, carry out steps 3–4 below.

In the next stage in the Interview, you tell QuickBooks UK whether you want to set up any Other Charges items. Other Charges items relate to miscellaneous expenses (e.g. postage and delivery) which are otherwise unclassifiable.

Carry out step 1 below if you don't need to set up an Other Charges item (however, see the Remember tip on the left if you do), then carry out step 2:

| Click here

2 Click here

Now perform steps 3–4 below (but see the Handy Tip on the left if you want to create additional Other Charges items):

HANDY TIP

Re step 3 – if you want to create further items, click Yes. Now follow the appropriate steps above.

Repeat this as often as necessary. When you've created enough items, follow steps 3–4 on the right.

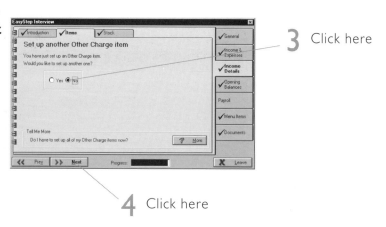

3 Click here

4 Click here

Click Next in the subsequent window to complete the Items topic.

The Income Details tab (8)

In the final topic in the Income Details section, you give QuickBooks UK details of stock items (i.e. items you keep for some time before selling). QuickBooks needs to know:

- the item's name or numerical reference

- the name of the income account you want the item associated with

Additionally, it's a very good idea to supply:

- the number of items currently held in stock

- the total value of items currently held in stock

You can also supply the following information, if you want:

- helpful descriptions

- the number of items (the 'reorder point') at which you want QuickBooks to prompt you to reorder

- cost details

If you indicated earlier in Interview that you don't keep stock, the Stock topic is inactive.

Adding stock items

Click Next in the first Stock topic window, then do the following:

Click here

2 Click here

The Income Details tab (9)

Now carry out the following steps, as appropriate:

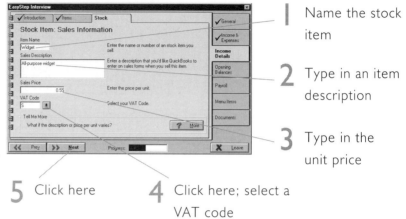

**Re step 6 –
select the
income
account
which best reflects
the income
generated when you
sell the stock item.
If none of the
existing income
accounts is suitable,
you can create a
new one on-the-fly.**
   **Choose <Add
New> in the list. The
New Account dialog
launches; complete
this, then click OK.
Finally, follow steps
7–11.**

I   Name the stock
item

2   Type in an item
description

3   Type in the
unit price

5   Click here

4   Click here; select a
VAT code

6   Click here;
select an
income account
in the list

7   Click here

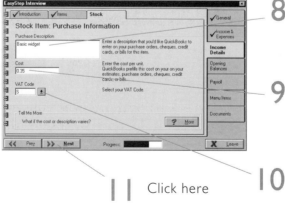

8   Type in a
purchase
description

9   Type in the
purchase unit
price

10   Click here;
select a VAT
code

11   Click here

The Income Details tab (10)

Carry out the following steps:

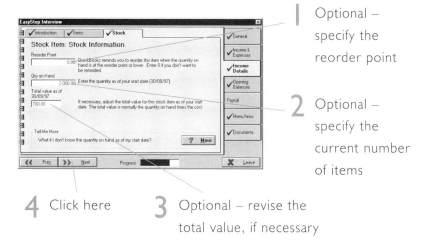

1 Optional – specify the reorder point

2 Optional – specify the current number of items

4 Click here

3 Optional – revise the total value, if necessary

HANDY TIP

Re step 5 – if you want to create further stock items, click Yes instead. Now follow the appropriate steps on page 52, and above.

Repeat this as often as necessary. When you've created enough items, follow steps 5–6 on the right.

Now perform steps 5–6 below (but see the Handy Tip on the left if you want to create additional stock items):

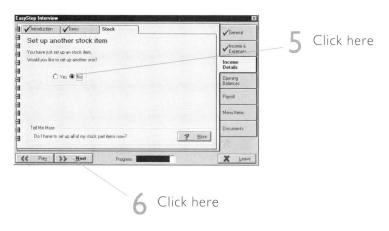

5 Click here

6 Click here

Click the Next button in the subsequent window; this completes the Income Details section.

The Opening Balances tab (1)

Your balance sheet indicates the *ongoing* value of your business by comparing assets (e.g. bank accounts and money owed to you) and liabilities (e.g. credit cards and loans).

QuickBooks UK also includes equity accounts. (Equity is defined as assets minus liabilities.)

If you have any trouble collating this information, consider any of the following:
- **changing the start date**
- **extrapolating amounts owed to you (by subtracting payments made and adding orders placed)**
- **making intelligent guesses**

If you need to guess, don't worry: you can change entries later.

You use the Opening Balances section to enter:

- details of customers and vendors who owe you money

- details of your balance sheet accounts

You'll need to have the following to hand before you begin:

- The bank statement which falls on or before your start date (selected when you used the Start Date tab in the General section of the Interview)

- details of your assets and liabilities

- details (names and amounts) of customers and vendors who owe you money

Starting the Opening Balances section

In the first three windows, click Next; this completes the Introduction topic. Click Next in the first window in the Customers topic. Now carry out steps 1–2 if you have customers who owed you money as at your start date:

Click here

2 Click here

If you *don't* have outstanding customers, select No in step 1 instead; in this scenario, following step 2 takes you directly to the Vendors topic on page 56.

The Opening Balances tab (2)

Now carry out the following steps:

Re step 1 – if you want to track customer projects (for instance, if you decide to monitor income/expenses for specific jobs), click Yes instead. Then follow steps 2–5. After this, complete the further two windows which launch.

Finally, carry out steps 6–7 below.

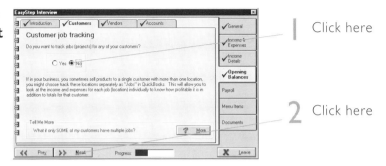

1 Click here

2 Click here

3 Enter the customer's name

4 Type in the outstanding amount

5 Click here

Re step 6 – if you want to create further customer entries, click Yes instead. Now follow the appropriate steps on page 54, and above.

Repeat this as often as necessary. When you've created enough items, follow steps 6–7 on the right.

Now perform steps 6–7 below (but see the Handy Tip on the left if you want to create additional customer entries):

6 Click here

7 Click here

Click the Next button in the subsequent window; this completes the Customers topic.

The Opening Balances tab (3)

REMEMBER

If no vendors owed you money, select No instead. Click Next. The final Vendors window launches; click Next to complete the topic.

HANDY TIP

If you want to add further outstanding vendors, click Yes instead. Now repeat the procedures just outlined. Repeat this as often as necessary. When you've created enough items, click No in the penultimate Vendors window; in the final window, click Next.

The Vendors topic

If you opted to pay and enter bills immediately (see step 3 on page 37), you don't need to track outstanding bills. For this reason, the Vendors topic in the Opening Balances section is inoperative. Simply go straight to page 57.

If, on the other hand, you elected to defer payment of bills, click Next in the first window in the Vendors topic. In the subsequent window, select Yes if – on your start date – there were any vendors to whom you owed money. Click Next. In the third window in the Vendors topic, type in the vendor's name and the amount owed, then click Next. In the fourth window, click No if there are no further outstanding vendors to enter (but see the Handy Tip on the left if there are), followed by Enter.

Click Next in the fifth window to complete the Vendors topic.

The Accounts topic

Use the Accounts topic to set up any of the following accounts:

- credit card

- loan

- bank

- asset

- equity

Click Next in the first Accounts window, then follow the steps on page 57.

The Opening Balances tab (4)

Setting up credit card accounts
Carry out the following steps:

 REMEMBER

Re step 1 – click No instead if you don't want to set up a credit card account. Carry out step 2. Then omit steps 3–7 below.

1 Click here

2 Click here

3 Enter the name of the card

4 Click here

 HANDY TIP

Re step 5 – enter the date of the last statement *on or before your start date.*

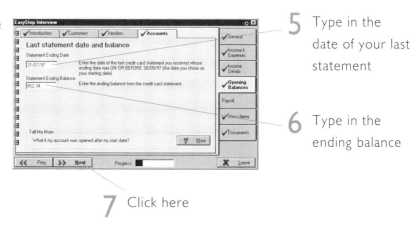

5 Type in the date of your last statement

6 Type in the ending balance

7 Click here

The Opening Balances tab (5)

Now carry out steps 1–2 below if you *don't* want to set up any additional credit card accounts (if you do, see the Handy Tip on the left):

Re step 1 – if you want to create further credit card accounts, click Yes instead. Now follow the appropriate steps on page 57.

Repeat this as often as necessary. When you've created enough items, follow steps 1–2 on the right.

Click here

2 Click here

Creating other accounts

To set up one or more loan, bank, asset and equity accounts, work through the remainder of the Accounts topic, using the steps on pages 57 (and above) as a template. (When you finish a window, click the Next button to move on the subsequent window.)

A further section – Payroll – is beyond the scope of this book.

Finally, click the Next button in the final window in the Accounts topic, then perform both of the following:

- complete the Opening Balances section.

- move on to the Menu Items section on page 59.

The Menu Items tab

HANDY TIP

You'll probably use the Lists and Activities menus frequently when you work with your new QuickBooks UK company, so it's worth taking the time to complete this section.

In the Menu Items section, you customise specific elements on the Lists and Activities menus.

Carry out the following steps:

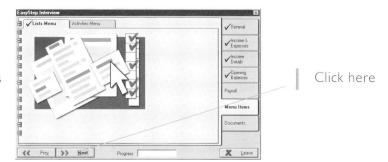

Click here

2 Click here

REMEMBER

Re step 3 – the To Do list displays tasks and reminders on the date specified:

Activating dates

Reminders

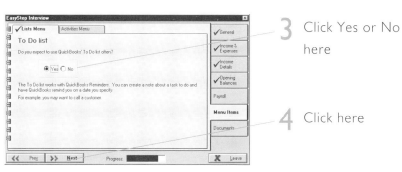

3 Click Yes or No here

4 Click here

Click the Next button in the subsequent window; this completes the Lists Menu topic.

Carry out the following steps to customise your Activities menu:

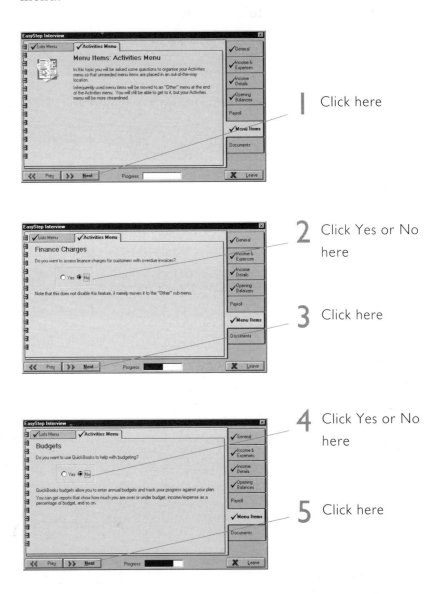

1 Click here

2 Click Yes or No here

3 Click here

4 Click Yes or No here

5 Click here

Click the Next button in the subsequent window; this completes the Menu Items section.

The Documents tab

The Documents topic in the Documents section provides access to five special Help documents. These cover the following topics:

- Entering historical transactions

- Handling petty cash

- Combining personal and business expenses

- Using QuickBooks for contact management

- Ordering QuickBooks supplies & services

All the supplied Help files are worth viewing; especially valuable is the 'Entering historical transactions' document (featured in the illustration below).

See the Handy Tip below for how to use the Help files.

Starting the Documents section

Click Next in the first two windows. Then carry out the following step:

Click this button to view the associated Help file:

Press Esc when you've finished using it.

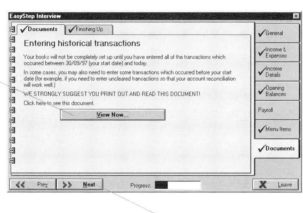

Click here

Four additional windows now launch, each offering access to a Help file. Follow the procedure in the Handy Tip on page 61 to view the file, then carry out step 1 on page 61.

In the final window in the Documents topic, do the following:

| Click here

Now do the following to complete the Documents section, and the EasyStep Interview:

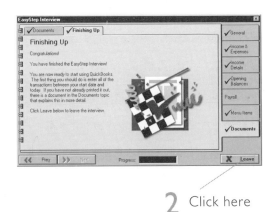

2 Click here

Accounts

In this chapter, you'll learn about QuickBooks UK's balance sheet and income/expense account types in some detail. You'll discover how to launch your Chart of Accounts; you'll also print it out, for an overview of your account structure. Then you'll create new accounts/subaccounts; rename, delete, merge and deactivate them; amend the account type; and rearrange your account order within your Chart of Accounts. Finally, you'll learn how to use account registers as an alternative way to enter data, and change the associated colours.

Chapter Three

Covers

Accounts – an overview

You can, however, number accounts if you want – see page 81.

QuickBooks UK adopts a far more flexible attitude towards accounts than most accounting software. Instead of the usual rigid account structure, and the assumption that accounts *must* be numbered, QuickBooks lets you do the following easily and conveniently:

- create new accounts (and name them with permutations of letters/numbers)

- rename accounts (or reorder them within your Chart of Accounts)

- change an account's type

Accounts monitor the flow of money in and out of your company.

- delete accounts

- merge accounts

Standard accounting practice groups accounts in a central Chart of Accounts; QuickBooks follows this precedent. In addition, accounts are divided into two overall categories:

- balance sheet accounts

- income and expense accounts

**Your Chart of Accounts is a centralised list of accounts. Balance sheet accounts precede income/ expense accounts.
  See pages 67–70 for how to use your Chart of Accounts.**

A balance sheet is a one-off snapshot of your financial situation *on a specific date*. It compares:

- assets (what you own and amounts owed to you)

- liabilities (what you owe to others)

- equity (your company's net worth)

Examples of balance sheet accounts are:

Asset	bank accounts, accounts receivable
Liability	accounts payable, credit card accounts
Equity	retained earnings

The illustration below shows a standard QuickBooks UK balance sheet:

Income and expense accounts track the sources of your company's income and the destination of expenditure, and are properly the province of a Profit and Loss (P&L) report. Unlike balance sheets, however, income and expense accounts operate over the current financial period.

REMEMBER

Note, however, that P&L reports can also figure – as a category in their own right – in balance sheets.

There is a tie-in between balance sheets and income and expense accounts. When you enter transactions into balance sheet accounts, you normally classify them under one or more income or expense accounts.

Examples of income and expense accounts are:

Cost of Goods Sold	the cost of stock held before sale
Income	normal business income

A standard P&L report (showing income and expense accounts)

At this stage, you should give some thought to which QuickBooks UK income and expense accounts you'll need to use.

Income accounts – more information

Consider the following question:

- How much detail do you require on your Profit and Loss reports?

If you don't need a lot of detail, you can make do with using just a few income accounts. If you need greater detail, use (or create) more.

As a general rule, income accounts are divided into two overall types:

Income	business-related income
Other income	non business-related income (e.g. interest)

Expense accounts – more information

Again, you may decide to use relatively few expense accounts, or you may require more detailed tracking of expenditure. As a general rule, however, you'll use more expense accounts than income accounts, because the more you use, the greater the control you'll have.

When you enter bills in QuickBooks UK, you apply one or more expense accounts to the transaction.

There are three overall expense account types:

Expense	business-related expenses
Cost of Goods Sold	cost of stock held
Other Expense	non business-related expenses

Your Chart of Accounts (1)

You can launch the Chart of Accounts window:

HANDY TIP **You can also use a keystroke shortcut: simply press Ctrl+A.**

- from within the QuickBooks Navigator

- via a menu route

Launching the Chart of Accounts – the Navigator route

Carry out the following:

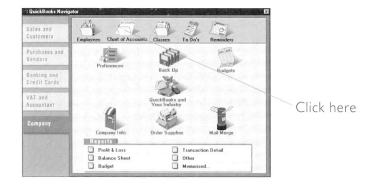

Click here

Launching the Chart of Accounts – the menu route

Pull down the Lists menu and carry out the following:

Click here

Your Chart of Accounts (2)

This is the result:

Associated Qcard
– see page 22

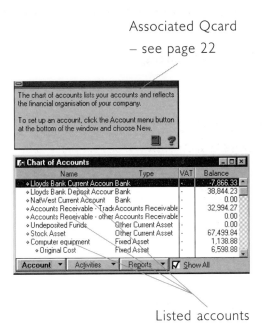

Listed accounts

Closing the Chart of Accounts

Carry out the following:

Click here

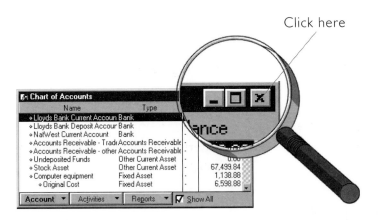

Your Chart of Accounts (3)

Printing the Chart of Accounts

You can print out a list of individual accounts from within the Chart of Accounts.

Do the following:

Click here

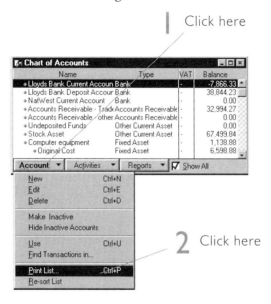

HANDY TIP

There are two aspects to every page size: a vertical measurement, and a horizontal measurement. These can be varied according to orientation. There are two possible orientations:

2 Click here

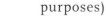

QuickBooks UK now launches a special dialog from which you can specify:

*   the printer you want to use

*   the page orientation

*   a page range (i.e. you can limit the print run to specific pages)

*   whether printing occurs in draft mode (for proofing purposes)

You can also:

*   preview your Chart of Accounts before printing

*   set printer options

 Portrait

 Landscape

Your Chart of Accounts (4)

To print a restricted page range, type in start and end numbers here:
Finally, carry out step 6 to begin printing.

If you need to adjust your printer's internal settings, click this button:

Now complete the dialog which launches, as appropriate. Finally, follow step 6 to begin printing.

Now carry out steps 1–5, as appropriate. Finally, perform step 6 to initiate printing:

Click here; select a printer in the list

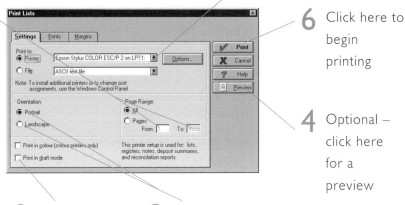

6 Click here to begin printing

4 Optional – click here for a preview

2 Click here to print in draft

3 Select an orientation

If you carried out step 4, the Print Preview window launches. Proof your Chart of Accounts, then carry out step 5 below. Finally, carry out step 6 above:

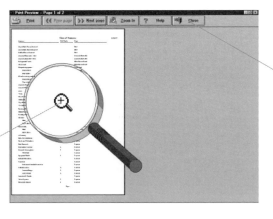

This is the Zoom cursor: left-click once to zoom in, again to zoom out

5 Click here to return to the Print Lists dialog

New accounts

QuickBooks UK, as a result of the information you supply during the EasyStep Interview (see Chapter Two), automates the setting up of your Chart of Accounts. In the course of doing this, it creates most of the accounts you'll need. However, there are situations where you may well wish to create your own accounts. For example, if you open a new bank account, you may wish to create a new QuickBooks balance sheet account...

REMEMBER **See page 72 for more about subaccounts.**

Additionally, you may decide to create subaccounts and apply them to a parent account, for the purpose of tracking income and expenses in more detail.

Creating a new account

First launch the Chart of Accounts (see page 67 for how to do this). Then do the following:

Click here

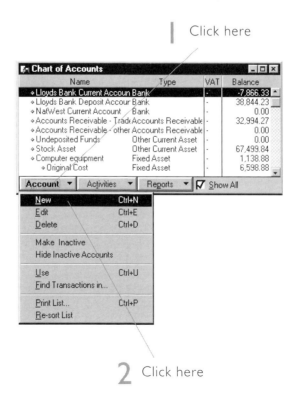

2 Click here

...contd

Re step 2 – you can use letters, numbers or combinations of both.

Now complete the New Account dialog, using the following steps as a guide. (To some extent, the account type you select in step 1 determines which fields are present in the dialog.)

1 Click here; in the list, select an account type

If you want, you can also do the following:
- **type in descriptive detail here:**
- **type in the account number here:**

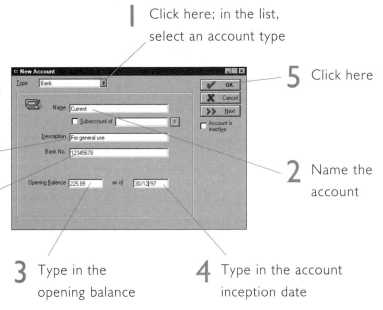

5 Click here

2 Name the account

3 Type in the opening balance

4 Type in the account inception date

Subaccounts

It's sometimes useful to set up 'child' accounts (QuickBooks UK calls these 'subaccounts') under an overall 'parent' account. For instance, QuickBooks may have automatically included a Fixed Asset account called 'Computer equipment' in your Chart of Accounts. If it's helpful to you to itemise your equipment over more than one site, you could set up subaccounts relating to the separate premises.

After steps A and B, carry out steps 3–5 above, as appropriate.

To set up a subaccount, carry out steps 1–2 above, then do the following in the New Account dialog:

A Click here   B Click here; select a parent account

Account housekeeping (1)

QuickBooks UK lets you edit existing accounts in various ways. You can:

- change the account's title

- change the account type (and other associated information e.g. account numbers)

HANDY TIP

You can also recolour account registers – see page 84.

- delete the account (but only in certain circumstances – see later)

- merge accounts (but only in certain circumstances – see later)

- rearrange the order of accounts within your Chart of Accounts

- make accounts inactive

Renaming accounts

First launch your Chart of Accounts (for how to do this, see page 67). Now do the following:

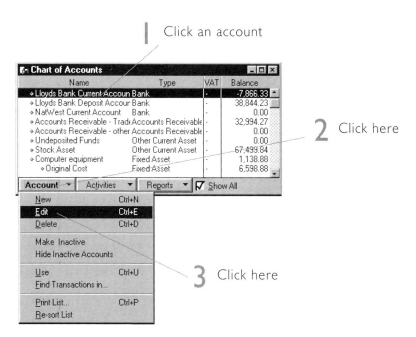

Click an account

2 Click here

3 Click here

Account housekeeping (2)

Now carry out the following steps:

Type in a new name

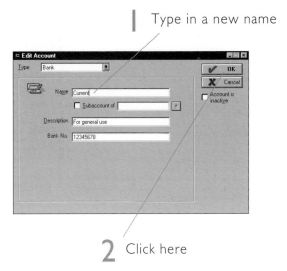

2 Click here

Re 1 – you can, however, detach any associated subaccounts, and _then_ amend the parent account's type.

Re 5 – when you perform certain actions for the first time (e.g. entering a bill or creating an invoice), QuickBooks creates a new account automatically.

Changing the account type

QuickBooks UK makes it easy to change account types, but the process is subject to the following restrictions:

1. you can't allocate a new type to accounts which have associated subaccounts (but see the Handy Tip)

2. you can't allocate a new type to accounts which are classified as accounts payable and accounts receivable

3. you can't transform existing accounts into accounts receivable or accounts payable accounts

4. you can't allocate a new type to Bank accounts

5. you can't allocate a new type to accounts which are automatically created _during your use of QuickBooks_ (see the Remember tip on the left)

See page 75 for how to amend account types.

Account housekeeping (3)

Changing the account type

To amend an account type, first launch your Chart of Accounts (for how to do this, see page 67). Now do the following:

Click an account

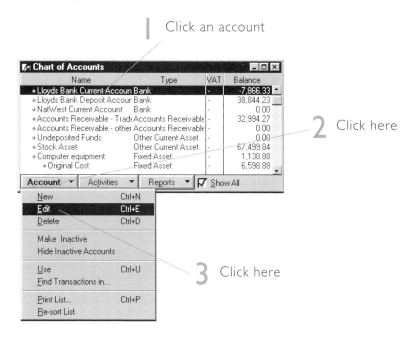

2 Click here

3 Click here

HANDY TIP **If you want to change other account information (e.g. the description), simply amend the relevant fields before you carry out step 5.**

4 Click here; in the list, select an account type

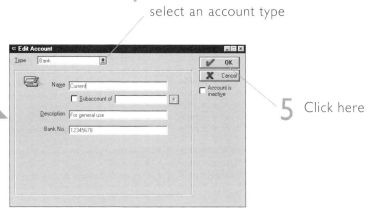

5 Click here

Account housekeeping (4)

Re 1 – to delete an account with transactions, you have to reallocate each transaction to a new account first.

Re 2 – to delete an account with one or more associated subaccounts, you have to delete the subaccount(s) first.

Deleting accounts

You can only delete an account if:

1. it has not been applied to any transactions

2. no subaccounts have been associated with it

3. no line items have been associated with it (line items are services or products which are itemised on invoices, purchase orders or bills)

To delete an account or subaccount, first launch your Chart of Accounts (for how to do this, see page 67). Now do the following:

Click an account
or subaccount

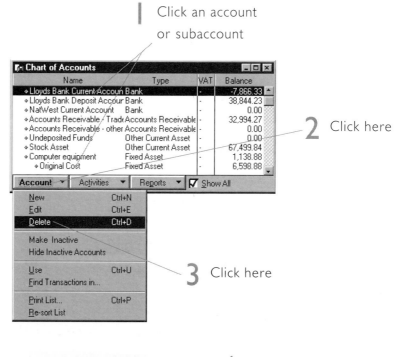

2 Click here

3 Click here

If you attempt to delete an account or subaccount which can't be deleted, a special message appears after step 3. Do the following to return to your Chart of Accounts:

4 Click here

Click here

Account housekeeping (5)

Merging accounts

QuickBooks lets you amalgamate ('merge') two accounts into one, subject to the following:

- the accounts must have the same type

- if you're merging two subaccounts, both must have the same parent account

To merge two accounts, first launch your Chart of Accounts (for how to do this, see page 67). Now do the following:

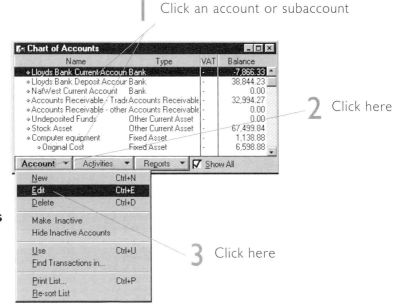

Click an account or subaccount

2 Click here

3 Click here

HANDY TIP

This means you can use the merging process as a way of deleting unwanted accounts.

The account selected in step 1 is absorbed into the account you select in step 1 on page 78 and is, in effect, deleted.

Carry out the additional steps on page 78 to complete the merge process.

Account housekeeping (6)

Merging accounts

The Edit Account dialog now launches (some of the fields vary according to the account type).

Carry out the following additional steps:

2 Click here

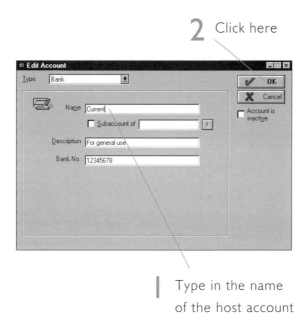

Type in the name
of the host account

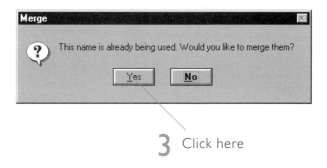

3 Click here

Account housekeeping (7)

Rearranging accounts

By default, QuickBooks orders its accounts within your Chart of Accounts:

•   by account type

•   alphabetically, within each type

However, you can manually alter the order, to suit your own requirements.

First launch your Chart of Accounts (for how to do this, see page 67). Now do the following:

HANDY TIP

Re step 1 – **you can also rearrange the order of subaccounts within their parent account.**

> Move the mouse pointer over the diamond to the left of the account you want to move

After step 1 above, the cursor changes to a four-pronged arrow.

Now drag the account to its new location within your Chart of Accounts. Finally, release the mouse button to confirm the move.

Account housekeeping (8)

If your Chart of Accounts is large, with a lot of entries, it's often helpful to hide individual accounts which you don't often use.

QuickBooks calls this process 'making accounts inactive'. When you do this, none of the data associated with the inactive accounts is discarded; the only result is that your Chart of Accounts is less cluttered.

Making accounts inactive

Within your Chart of Accounts, do the following:

 When you deactivate an account, it's prefixed with

in your Chart of Accounts.
  However, it's only visible if this box: is selected (i.e. it contains ✔).

Click an account or subaccount

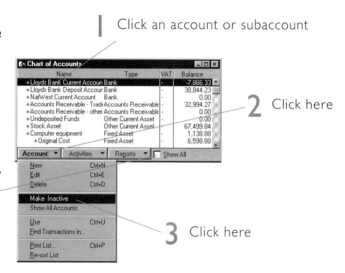

2 Click here

3 Click here

Making accounts active

Carry out steps 1–2 above. Now do the following in the sub-menu which launches:

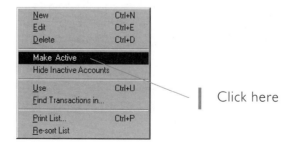

Click here

Account numbering

We saw on page 72 that you can use any mixture of letters and/or numbers in account names. For many users, this will be the preferred way of identifying accounts. However, if you want you can also number accounts separately.

When you've turned on account numbering (see below), an additional field appears in the appropriate dialog when you:

- create new accounts

- amend existing accounts

The Numbers field, added (here) to the New Account dialog

Type a number in the Numbers field, then complete the remainder of the dialog. Finally, click OK.

Turning on account numbering

Pull down the File menu and click Preferences. Do the following:

Click here

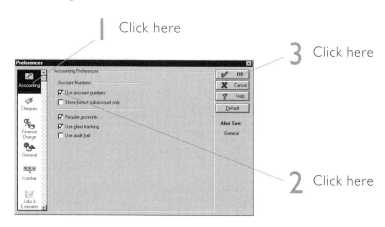

3 Click here

2 Click here

Using account registers

There are advantages to using the register directly: it's quicker, and you have a useful overview of neighbouring transactions.

Normally, you enter transactions in QuickBooks UK without reference to the underlying account. For example, when you enter a bill, you do so in a special window (the Enter Bills window); QuickBooks itself automatically enters details into the appropriate accounts payable register. However, if you want you can enter certain transaction types into a special window which provides *direct* access to the account; QuickBooks calls this the 'register'.

You can enter:

- simple bills directly into an accounts payable register

You can also amend some existing account transactions via the register.
For example, in liability, asset and equity accounts, you can enter adjustments.

- new cheques and deposits into Bank accounts

- new charges/credits into credit card accounts

Launching an account's register

First launch your Chart of Accounts (for how to do this, see page 67). Now do the following:

Double-click an account or subaccount

If you can't find the account you want, make sure this is selected:

...contd

The account register now appears. Carry out the following steps:

2 Click a transaction

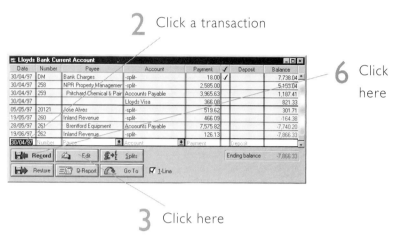

6 Click here

3 Click here

HANDY TIP

For more information on how to complete the data entry forms which launch after step 3, see later chapters.

QuickBooks now launches a 'data entry form'; which form appears depends on the account type chosen in step 1 on page 82. In the example below, the Write Cheques form has appeared as a result of carrying out steps 2–3 above in respect of a Bank account transaction.

Carry out steps 4–5 below, then 6 above:

REMEMBER

As yet, this form shows no transaction details because (in this instance) step 2 selected the next *blank* transaction.

Following steps 2–3 in respect of an already entered transaction results in the existing details being inserted in the dialog.

4 Complete the form

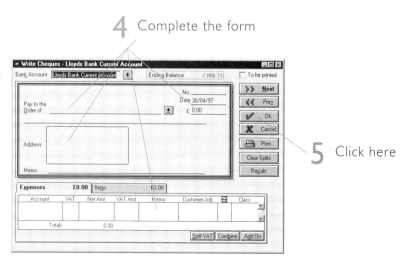

5 Click here

Account colours

REMEMBER

Changing an account's colour also redesigns any associated data entry forms (e.g. the Write Cheques dialog on page 83).

QuickBooks UK lets you change the colour associated with a given account's register.

This is particularly useful if you have numerous accounts of the same type. To avoid confusion (e.g. entering a cheque in the wrong account), you can allocate a different colour to each.

Changing an account's colour

First launch your Chart of Accounts (for how to do this, see page 67). Now do the following:

Double-click an account

HANDY TIP

If you can't find the account you want, make sure this is selected:

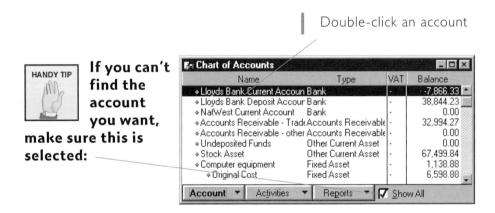

The account's register launches. Pull down the Edit menu and click Change Account Colour. Now do the following:

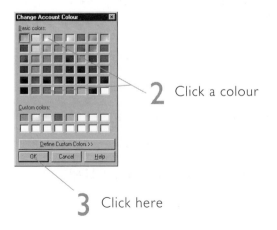

2 Click a colour

3 Click here

Sales

This chapter shows you how to enter sales forms (invoices, cash sales and credit memos). You'll learn about invoice formats, and how to enter refunds/returns. You'll also record cheques for (and connect them to) returns. You'll preview sales forms, and then go on to print them, singly or in groups. Finally, you'll mark sales as pending; create daily cash sale summaries; void/delete sales; and create and recall memorised sales forms.

Chapter Four

Covers

Sales – an overview

Every time you sell a product/service, you need to give QuickBooks UK details of the transaction. You do this, conveniently and accurately, by completing and posting a sales form.

Types of sales form

QuickBooks uses three basic sales forms:

Invoices

use these to have QuickBooks record sales transactions which result in money owed to you by a customer. (Invoices are automatically entered in an accounts receivable account).

Cash sales

when you receive payment for an order then-and-there, use a cash sales form. You can enter credit card and cheque payments, as well as cash amounts

Credit memos

use these to record returns and order cancellations for products/services which have already been the subject of payment

All three sales types are entered into QuickBooks UK by means of special windows. For example, you use the Enter Cash Sales window to record cash sales...

The Enter Cash Sales window

Invoice formats

QuickBooks UK provides three principal invoice formats:

- Service

- Professional

- Product

These formats relate, primarily, to the kind of business you carry out. Intuit suggests you use:

- Service if your business is largely service-orientated (as opposed to product-orientated)

- Professional if your business is largely service-orientated AND the services you offer require a lot of description

- Product if your business deals principally with stock or parts

See page 88 for illustrations of the above formats.

In addition, you can – if you want – customise your own invoice layout, although many users (because the existing formats are so detailed) won't need to do this. See page 89 for more information.

During the course of the EasyStep Interview, you selected a default invoice format. However, when you generate an invoice you can easily select another.

Choosing a format

If it isn't immediately obvious which format you should use, consider the following:

- How detailed do you want your invoices to be?

In particular, decide how long you want each individual line item (the entry for each service or product you sell) to be. When you've decided these two points, selecting an invoice format is much easier.

...contd

Invoice formats

Compare the following:

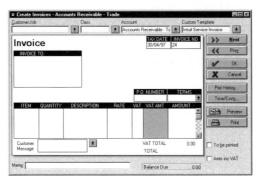

The Service format – the Item field is omitted in printed versions, giving more room for descriptions

HANDY TIP

When all three formats are printed, certain fields (because they're reserved for internal use) do not appear.

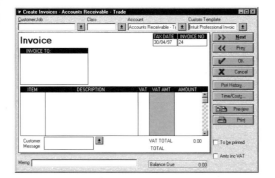

The Professional format – again, the Item field is omitted when printed, but also has the largest Descriptions field

HANDY TIP

You can preview invoices before you print them. See page 99.

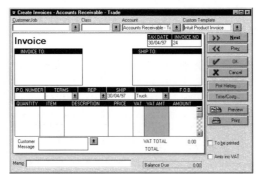

The Product format – has the most fields when printed, and the smallest Descriptions field

Entering invoices – initial steps

HANDY TIP

To create your own invoice format, refer to the Create Invoices window on page 90. Click the arrow to the right of the Custom Template field; in the box, select Customise.

In the Select a Template field in the Customise Template dialog, click Customised Invoice. Click Edit. Work through the tabs in the Customise Invoice dialog, selecting and naming the fields you want to appear.

Finally, back in the Create Invoices window, click the arrow to the right of the Custom Template field; in the box, select Customised Invoice. Complete the rest of the window (see pages 90–94 for how to do this).

You enter invoices through the Create Invoices window. You can launch this in two ways:

The menu route

Pull down the Activities menu and do the following:

Click here

The Navigator route

Carry out the following steps:

Click here

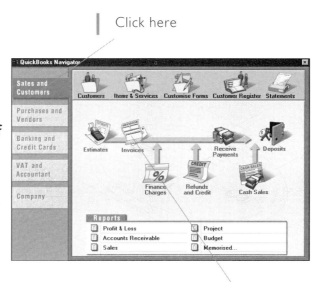

2 Click here

Entering invoices – stage 1

REMEMBER

Re step 1 – the Accounts field is only operative if you have more than one accounts receivable account.

Now complete the Create Invoices window. There are three stages to this process. In the first, you complete the customer section of the window

Perform steps 1–4 below:

2 Click here; select a job

1 Click here; select an accounts receivable account

HANDY TIP

To change the invoice format, click the arrow to the right of the Custom Template field; in the box, select a new format.

Selecting a new format varies, to some extent, the fields contained in the Create Invoices window.

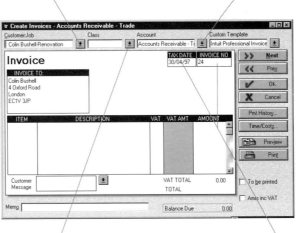

3 Click here; select a class

4 Optional – change the date or invoice number

HANDY TIP

Re step 2 – selecting a job inserts the associated address into the INVOICE TO: field (and also the SHIP TO: field, if the invoice format is Product).

More help with stage 1

Step 2 above

QuickBooks UK maintains a list of customers and/or jobs; completing this field is mandatory. If none of the existing customers/jobs are applicable, select <Add New> in the list. Now carry out steps 1–3 on page 91.

...contd

Complete steps 1–3 to create a new customer/job:

If necessary, complete the remainder of this dialog.
Click these tabs then complete the additional fields. Finally, carry out step 3.

Type in the client's name

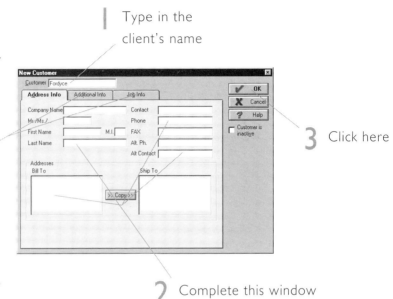

3 Click here

2 Complete this window

Re the Handy Tip above – clicking the Job Info tab allows you to create (and therefore track) jobs under the aegis of a specific customer.

More help with stage 1

Step 3 on page 90

This field is inoperative if – in the course of the EasyStep Interview – you did not opt to use QuickBooks classes. If none of the existing classes are applicable, select <Add New> in the list. Now carry out steps A and B below:

You can create subclasses, too.
Follow step A to name the new subclass. Click here: Now click here: In the list, select a host class. Lastly, perform step B.

A Name the new class

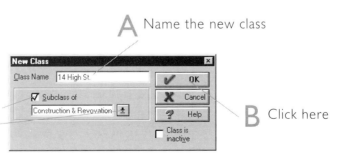

B Click here

Entering invoices – stage 2

In stage 2 in the invoice-completion process, you enter item information.

Perform steps 1–4 below:

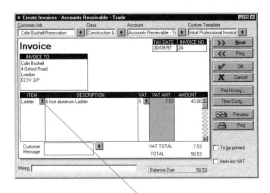

Click here; select an item in the list

More help with stage 2

Step 1 above

Items represent objects you sell or services you provide. QuickBooks UK maintains a list of items (you will have entered some in the EasyStep Interview). If none of the existing items are applicable, select <Add New> in the list. Now carry out steps 1–3 below:

HANDY TIP

Re step 2 – the fields within this dialog depend on the item type chosen in step 1. Complete them as appropriate.

Click here; select an item type

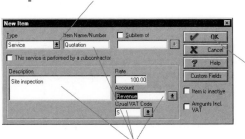

3 Click here

2 Complete the remaining fields

Entering invoices – stage 3

In the third and final stage in the invoice-completion process, you enter sales information.

Note, however, that none of the fields in the sales section of the Create Invoices dialog *have* to be completed: the information they can contain is merely useful.

Perform steps 1–3 below, as appropriate:

Click here; select a message

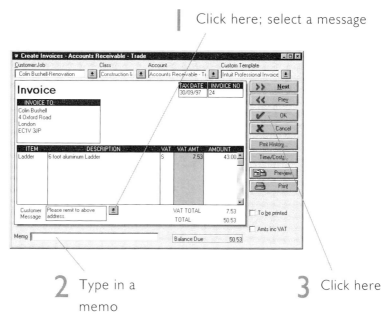

2 Type in a memo

3 Click here

More help with stage 3

Step 1 above

QuickBooks UK maintains an internal list of messages which have already been entered. If none of the existing messages are applicable, select <Add New> in the list. Now turn to page 94.

Now carry out the following steps to create a new message:

Type in your message

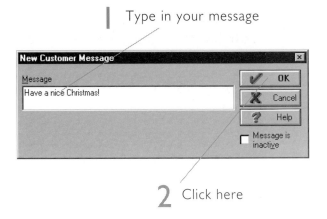

2 Click here

Step 2 on page 93

You can enter a one-off message (called a 'memo') here. Memos:
— do not appear on the printed versions of invoices
— do appear on printed statements
— do appear within accounts receivable registers
— do appear within relevant reports

Step 3 on page 93

After you carry out step 3, QuickBooks UK records the invoice in the selected accounts receivable account.

Entering cash sales

You enter cash and credit card sales through the Enter Cash Sales window. You can launch this in two ways:

The menu route
Pull down the Activities menu and do the following:

Click here

The Navigator route
Carry out the following steps:

Click here

2 Click here

Now carry out the following steps, as appropriate:

3 Click here;
select a client

2 Click here;
select a class

1 Click here; select
a template

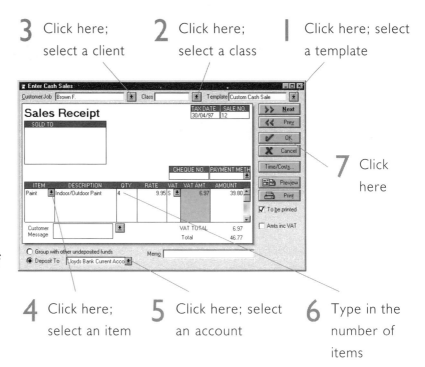

HANDY TIP **Complete the Customer Message and Memo fields, if appropriate. (See pages 93–94 for how to do this.)**

7 Click here

4 Click here;
select an item

5 Click here; select
an account

6 Type in the number of items

More help with cash sales

Step 2 above	This is optional. If none of the classes are applicable, follow steps A and B on page 91 to create and apply a new class
Step 3 above	This is optional. If none of the clients are applicable, follow steps 1–3 on page 91 to create and apply a new customer/job
Step 7 above	After you carry out step 7, QuickBooks UK records the cash or credit card sale in the account selected in step 5

Entering credit memos

You enter returns through the Create Credit Memos/ Refunds window. You can launch this in two ways:

 Use the Create Credit Memos/ Refunds window to enter returns in either of the following situations:

- **stock items are returned after a payment has already been recorded**
- **orders are cancelled after a payment has already been recorded**

The menu route
Pull down the Activities menu and do the following:

Click here

The Navigator route
Carry out the following steps:

Click here

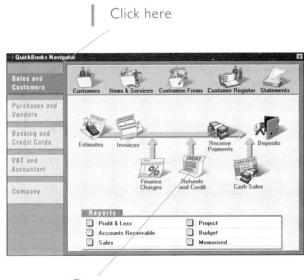

2 Click here

...contd

 Complete the Customer Message and Memo fields, if appropriate. (See pages 93–94.)

Now carry out the following steps, as appropriate:

2 Click here; select a client

1 Click here; select a class

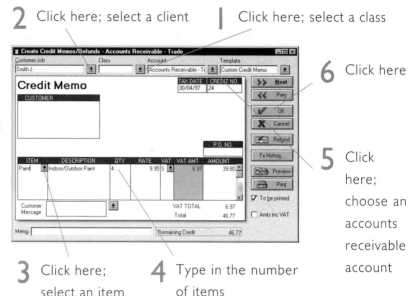

6 Click here

5 Click here; choose an accounts receivable account

 To record a cheque for the return, click the Refund button. The Write Cheques dialog launches:

Make sure the details are correct. Click OK. Or click Print to print the cheque (then complete the dialogs which launch.)

3 Click here; select an item

4 Type in the number of items

More help with cash sales

Step 1 above — This field is optional. If none of the classes are applicable, follow steps A and B on page 91 to create and apply a new class

Step 2 above — This field must be completed. If none of the existing customers/jobs are applicable, select <Add New> in the list. Now carry out steps 1–3 on page 91

Step 6 above — After you carry out step 6, QuickBooks UK records the return in the account selected in step 5

 To connect a refund cheque with its credit memo, see the Handy Tip on page 99.

Previewing sales forms

To connect the refund cheque to the credit memo you created on page 98, pull down the Activities menu and click Receive Payments. Complete the Receive Payments dialog. Particularly:
- **click the arrow to the right of the Customer:Job field and select the client**
- **ensure Apply Existing Credits is ticked**
- **ensure the refund entry at the base of the window is ticked**
- **(if appropriate) enter the amount of the credit in the Payment column Finally, click OK.**

In any of the following:

- the Create Invoices window

- the Enter Cash Sales window

- the Create Credit Memos/Refunds window

you can preview your sales form before you print it. This is especially useful in the Create Invoices window because of a discrepancy between the fields you see here and those which are reflected in the printed version.

Previewing a sales form

Within any of the windows listed above, click this button:

Now do the following when you've finished proofing your sales form:

This is the Zoom cursor: left-click once to zoom in, again to zoom out.

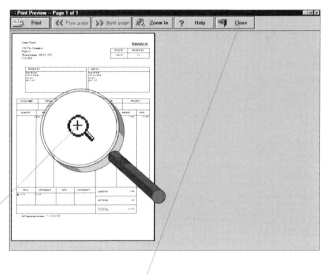

A previewed invoice

Click here

Printing sales forms

 If your sales forms don't print with the correct alignment, click the Align button in the dialog below. Complete the dialogs which launch, following the on-screen instructions.

You can print sales forms in two ways:

- singly, from within the Create Invoices, Enter Cash Sales and Create Credit Memos/Refunds windows

- in groups, from within a separate dialog

Printing sales forms singly

Launch the windows in the normal way (see pages 89, 95 and 97 for how to do this). Click this button:

 Re step 2 – choose 'Page-oriented' to print to laser or inkjet printers, or Continuous to print to dot matrix printers.

Now carry out the following steps, as appropriate:

2 Click here; select a printer type

1 Click here; select a printer in the list

6 Click here to begin printing

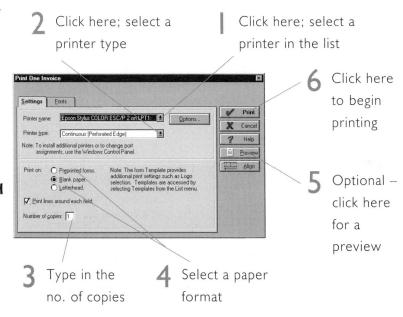

 If you need to adjust your printer's internal settings, click this button:

5 Optional – click here for a preview

3 Type in the no. of copies

4 Select a paper format

Now complete the dialog(s) which launch, as appropriate. Finally, follow step 6 to begin printing.

Step 5 launches the Print Preview window; for how to use this, see page 99.

...contd

You can't print cash sales forms in groups.

Ensure your printer is on-line and switched on (and that there is enough paper in it) before you begin printing.

To list a sales form in this dialog, first select this field:

in the Create Invoices or Create Credit Memos/ Refunds window *before* you follow the procedures here.

Printing sales forms in groups

Pull down the File menu and do the following:

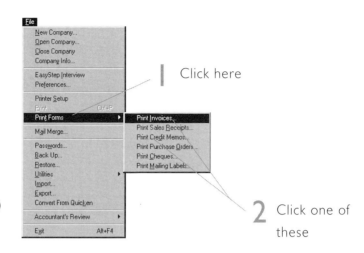

Click here

2 Click one of these

Now complete the following steps:

3 Click here; select a balance sheet account

4 Click as many sales forms as you want to print (a ✔ appears against each)

5 Click here

After step 3, QuickBooks launches an additional dialog – follow steps 1–6 on page 100.

Pending sales

QuickBooks UK lets you mark invoices, cash sales and credit memos as 'pending'. This means that the relevant transactions are not, as yet, reflected in account balances, reports and account registers.

Marking a sale as pending

From within the Create Invoices, Enter Cash Sales or Create Credit Memos/Refunds windows, pull down the Edit menu and do the following:

HANDY TIP **To mark the sale as final, pull down the Reports menu and click Sales Reports, Pending Sales. QuickBooks launches the Pending Sales Report:**

Double-click the relevant pending transaction; the associated sales form window appears, displaying the transaction. Pull down the Edit menu and click Mark ... As Final (where ... denotes the type of sales form). Click OK.

Finally, press Esc to close the report.

Click here

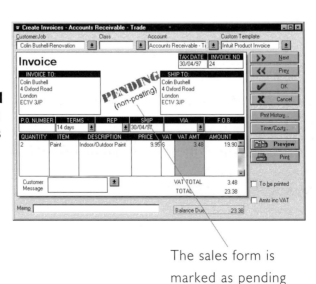

The sales form is marked as pending

Daily sales summaries

Ensure the Tax Date field contains the correct date.

On pages 95–96, you entered cash sales on an as-and-when basis. However, QuickBooks UK also lets you enter a summary of cash sales, at the end of the day. This is particularly useful if you don't need – or want – to allocate a customer/job to each sale.

Follow one of the procedures on page 95 to launch the Enter Cash Sales window. Now do the following:

If you're entering more than one cash sales total for different item types, enter details of the items here in the normal way. In step 2, enter *individual* **totals.**
   Now select this: instead of carrying out step 3. Finally, carry out step 4.

Click here; select Custom Cash Sale

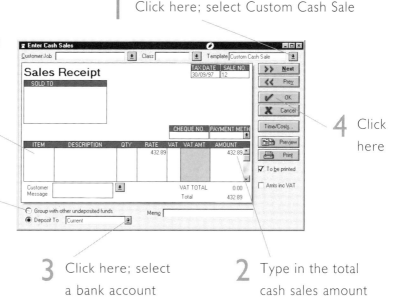

4 Click here

3 Click here; select a bank account

2 Type in the total cash sales amount

If you want to view this account, press Ctrl+A. Double-click this entry in your Chart of Accounts:
Undeposited Funds

After step 4, QuickBooks UK enters the cash sales summary into the bank account selected in step 3 (unless you followed the procedure in the Handy Tip, in which case the details are entered in a special account called 'Undeposited Funds').

Sales housekeeping

You'll probably need to void or delete sales at some time. However, you should be clear about the difference.

Voiding

Voiding ensures that the sale has no effect on the applicable account register. However, it still appears; QuickBooks simply:

• resets all sales form amounts to zero

• inserts VOID in the register's Memo field

See the illustration below:

An accounts receivable register with a voided transaction

Deleting

Deletion is a much more drastic measure. When you delete a sales form, it's gone for good.

Do not delete an invoice if either of the following situations apply:

• you've already applied a partial or full payment to it (see Chapter Seven). Instead, follow the procedures on pages 97–98 to create an appropriate credit memo entry

• you've made an error on it. Instead, simply correct and print the original sales form

...contd

To locate an existing invoice, cash sale

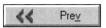

or refund, click this button:

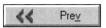

within the Create Invoices, Enter Cash Sales or Create Credit Memos/ Refunds window until you locate it.

Voiding a sale

Display the invoice, cash sale or refund you want to void (see the Handy Tip for how to do this). Then pull down the Edit menu and do the following (the precise menu entry depends on the type of sales form):

Click here

After step 1 on the right, a special message launches. Do the following:

Click here

Deleting a sale

Display the invoice, cash sale or refund you want to delete. Then pull down the Edit menu and do the following (the precise menu entry depends on the type of sales form):

Click here

Memorising sales forms

As well as sales forms, you can memorise most QuickBooks transactions (e.g. loan repayments or utilities payments) by selecting them within the register of the host account and then following the procedures listed here.

You can have QuickBooks UK memorise invoices, cash sales or credit memos. When you do so, it adds them to a special list: the Memorised Transaction list.

The advantage of memorising transactions is that you can have QuickBooks:

- insert them automatically, at a frequency you specify

- remind *you* to insert them

Memorising a sales form

From within the Create Invoices, Enter Cash Sales and Create Credit Memos/Refunds windows, pull down the Edit menu and do the following:

Click here

Re step 3 – select Remind Me to have QuickBooks UK remind you when a memorised invoice is due, or Standing Order to have it entered automatically.

2 Optional – rename the memorised sales form

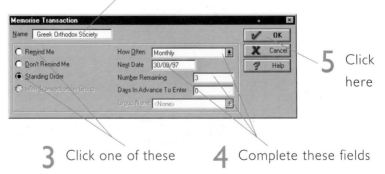

3 Click one of these   4 Complete these fields

5 Click here

...contd

Once a sales form has been memorised, you can tell QuickBooks UK to insert it into the relevant account; this process is called 'recalling'.

Recall memorised sales forms if you opted for the Remind Me option in step 3 on page 106.

Recalling a sales form

Pull down the Lists menu and do the following:

You can also recall other memorised transactions (e.g. loan repayments or utilities payments) by selecting them within the relevant account register and then following the procedures listed here.

Click here

2 Click a memorised sales form

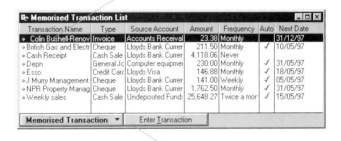

3 Click here

After step 3, QuickBooks UK launches the Create Invoices, Enter Cash Sales or Create Credit Memos/Refunds window, as appropriate. Make any necessary changes, then click OK to enter the sales form.

...contd

Once you've memorised a sales form, you can amend the details subsequently, if you want.

To delete a memorised sales form, follow step 1 on the right. Press Ctrl+D. Now do the following:

Editing a memorised sales form

Follow step 1 on page 107. Now do the following:

Click here

1 Click a memorised sales form

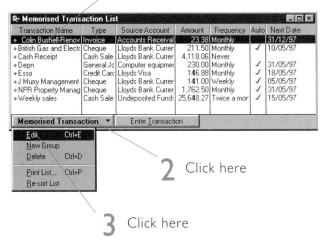

2 Click here

3 Click here

The procedures listed on this page also apply to other types of memorised transaction.

Now carry out steps 4–6 below, as appropriate. Finally, perform step 7:

4 Optional – rename the memorised sales form

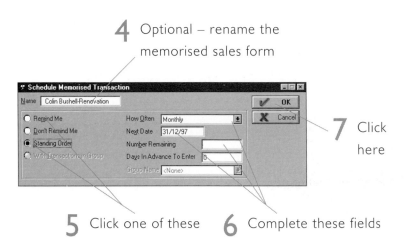

7 Click here

5 Click one of these

6 Complete these fields

Stock

This chapter helps you decide whether to use QuickBooks UK to track stock. You'll turn stock tracking on and off, and then create stock items. Once you've begun using the stock tracking feature, you'll view a list of outstanding purchase orders, and inspect ongoing stock items. Then you'll learn how to receive stock and process returns. Finally, you'll make manual adjustments to stock totals and view/use stock registers.

Chapter Five

Covers

Stock – an overview

If part of your business involves the following sequence:

- buying in parts/stock

- retaining them for a time

- reselling them subsequently

you can have QuickBooks UK track stock items for you.

When QuickBooks tracks an item, it maintains a note of the current number in hand (and returns this on request). It also monitors the current item value after sales.

In more detail, tracking stock in QuickBooks UK involves:

1. entering stock information on purchase orders (see Chapter Eight) and invoices or cash sales (see Chapter Four)

2. monitoring fluctuations in income following sales

3. monitoring fluctuations in COGS (Cost of Goods Sold) following sales or purchases

4. having QuickBooks return the average cost for any specified stock item

5. a warning from QuickBooks UK when you enter sales for items which are currently out of stock (although it doesn't prevent you from entering these sales)

QuickBooks uses three accounts to track stock:

Stock Asset	An asset account; tracks your stock's current value
Sales	An Income account; tracks the income from reselling stock
COGS	Tracks the cost to you of stock sales

REMEMBER

You may have added one or more stock items in the course of the EasyStep Interview (see Chapter Two, pages 51–53). However, you can easily add more items now – see pages 113–114.

Deciding whether to track stock

There are caveats to using QuickBooks UK to track stock. You shouldn't:

- track stock which has been subject to any kind of manufacturing process (because QuickBooks can't track *finished* goods). Additionally, QuickBooks can't:

  — provide details of the number of finished items

  — incorporate manufacturing labour costs

- use QuickBooks to track stock if you keep a large number of individual items (because entering transactions becomes unacceptably tedious after a given point). QuickBooks can track as many as 14,500 stock items, but the tedium threshold is considerably lower than this.

 All three methods of stock valuing are equally valid.
FIFO assumes that stock which is received first is used first; LIFO assumes that stock received last is used first; the Average Cost method (an attempt to take the middle ground) seeks to balance out the split.
If you have a rapid stock turnover, it may not matter much which method you use.

Additionally, QuickBooks uses a specific method for stock monitoring: the Average Cost method. This method (frequently used by accounting software) is one way of working out a value for each individual stock item. The overall goal is simple: arriving at the lower of cost and Net Realisable Value (the amount you would receive for the immediate sale of stock, less any associated costs).

There are, however, two other ways to arrive at overall stock values. If you want to use the LIFO (Last In First Out) or FIFO (First In First Out) methods – see the Remember tip – you should bear in mind that the figures QuickBooks produces *may* not be valid (although, having said this, many accountants are happy to receive figures which use the Average method)...

Stock tracking

When you worked through the EasyStep Interview, you will have decided whether or not to track stock. (See Chapter Two, page 35 for more information). However, you can reverse this at any time, if you want.

Turning on stock tracking

Pull down the File menu and do the following:

Click here

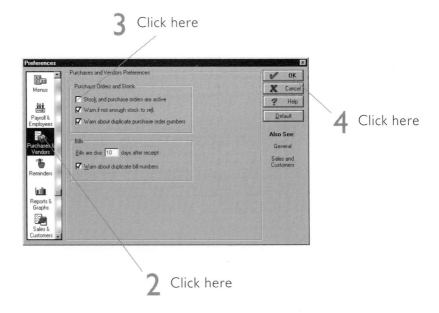

HANDY TIP

To turn off stock tracking, simply follows steps 1–4 again.

3 Click here

4 Click here

2 Click here

Creating stock items

You can add new stock items at any stage in your use of QuickBooks UK.

Adding a new stock item

Pull down the Lists menu and do the following:

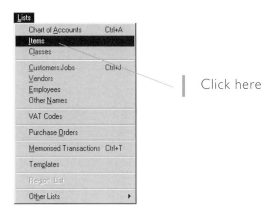

Click here

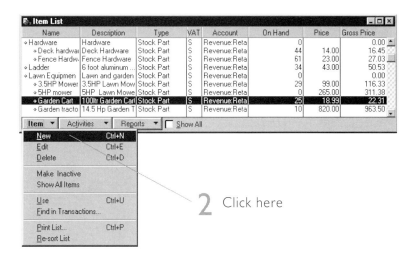

2 Click here

Now carry out the additional steps on page 114.

...contd

Carry out step 3 below:

3 Click here

HANDY TIP

Click the Amounts Incl. VAT field if you want the amounts you entered in steps 5 and 8 to include VAT.

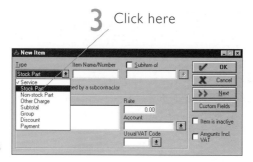

After step 3, the New Item dialog changes appropriately. Do the following:

HANDY TIP

Re step 9 – if you want to add more stock items, click the Next button instead.
  Now carry out steps 4–8 again. Perform step 9 when you've finished adding items.

4 Name the item

5 Type in the cost price

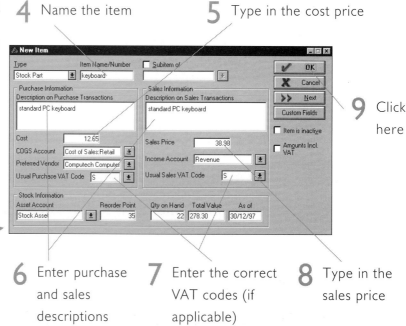

9 Click here

REMEMBER

You can also enter details of current stock levels (including the reorder point) in the fields here.

6 Enter purchase and sales descriptions

7 Enter the correct VAT codes (if applicable)

8 Type in the sales price

Viewing ordered items

Open purchase orders are purchase orders in which no payment has yet been received for at least one line item.

QuickBooks UK tracks which stock items have been ordered via purchase orders, and how many. You can view outstanding purchase orders in a dedicated list (see below), or you can inspect the stock items they contain (see page 116).

Listing purchase orders

QuickBooks displays purchase orders in a dedicated list. You can view all purchase orders, or just open ones.

Pull down the Lists menu and do the following:

For how to enter purchase orders, see Chapter Eight.

Click here

For how to enter sales, see Chapter Four.

For how to enter payments, see Chapter Seven.

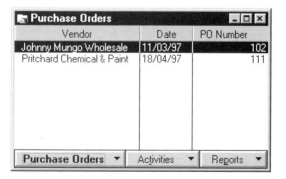

The Purchase Orders list – here, only open orders are displayed

To view *all* purchase orders, click this button:

In the menu, click Show All Purchase Orders.

...contd

 You can view a special report **which provides details of stock items (e.g. how many are at hand and how many are on order).**

Pull down the Reports menu and click Stock Reports, Stock Status by Item. This is the result:

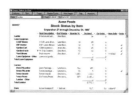

To close the report when you've finished using it, press Esc.

Inspecting stock items in purchase orders

Follow step 1 on page 115. Now carry out the following steps:

1 Click here

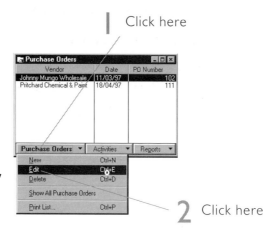

2 Click here

This is the result:

Stock items

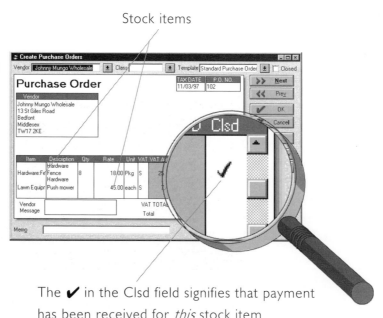

The ✔ in the Clsd field signifies that payment has been received for *this* stock item

Receiving stock

There are special procedures you need to follow when you receive stock deliveries. Which procedure you use depends on whether you:

- receive stock and then a bill

- receive stock and the bill at the same time

Receiving stock and the bill separately

If you used a purchase order to order the stock, pull down the Activities menu and do the following:

If you didn't use a purchase order to order the stock, omit step 3 here and steps 1–5 on page 118.

Instead, in the Create Item Receipts window, click the arrow to the right of the Vendor field; select a vendor. Complete the fields which describe the item near the base of the window.

Finally, click OK.

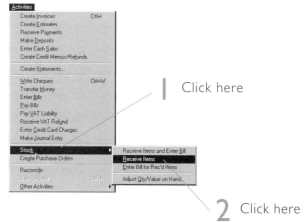

Click here

2 Click here

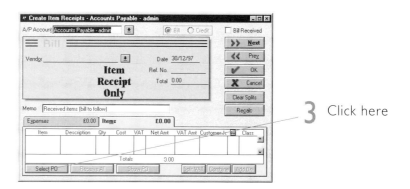

3 Click here

Now carry out the additional steps on page 118.

...contd

After step 5 (or after carrying out the procedures in the Handy Tip on page 117), do the following:

When you receive the bill, pull down the Activities menu and click Stock, Enter Bill for Rec'd Items. In the Vendor field in the Select Item Receipt dialog, select a vendor. Do the following:

B Click here

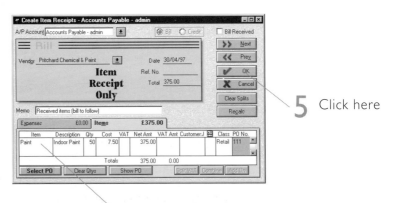

A Click an item receipt

The Enter Bills window launches; make any necessary amendments (in particular, ensure the amount due is the same as the bill total). Click OK. If a special message appears, click Yes.

Now carry out the following steps:

1 Click here; select a vendor

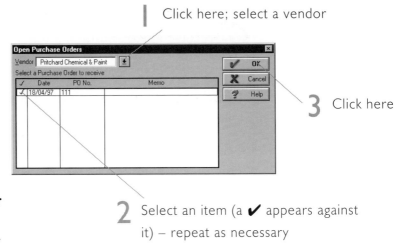

3 Click here

2 Select an item (a ✔ appears against it) – repeat as necessary

QuickBooks inserts the selected item(s) in the Create Item Receipts window. Now carry out the following steps:

5 Click here

4 QuickBooks has inserted the item selected in step 2; make any necessary amendments

Receiving stock and the bill simultaneously

Pull down the Activities menu and do the following:

Click here

2 Click here

The Enter Bills window launches – see below. Do one of the following:

- if you ordered the received stock by purchase order, carry out step 3 on page 117 and steps 1–5 on page 118

- if you didn't order the received stock by purchase order, click the arrow to the right of the Vendor field; select a vendor. Complete the fields which describe the item near the base of the window. Finally, click OK.

The Enter
Bills
window

Returning stock items

If you're recording a return *before* entering a bill, don't follow steps 1–6 here. Instead, do the following.

In the Lists menu, click Purchase Orders. Select an open purchase order. Press Ctrl+E. In the Create Purchase Orders window, click in the Clsd column next to the returned item(s). Click OK.

QuickBooks has procedures for returning items to a vendor. If you're recording a return *after* entering a bill, pull down the Activities menu and carry out the following steps (otherwise, see the Handy Tip):

Click here

See Chapter Nine for more information on paying bills.

3 Click here; select a vendor

2 Click here

6 Click here

4 Click here

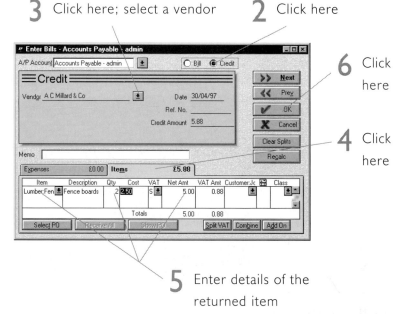

5 Enter details of the returned item

Manual stock adjustments

To view a stock item's average cost, click Item in the Lists menu. Select the item; press Ctrl+E. The Average cost is now displayed:

Qty on Hand	Avg. Cost	Qty on Order
22	12.65	0

Press Esc twice when you've finished.

Although QuickBooks automatically updates stock levels after each purchase and sale, it's sometimes necessary to adjust these manually (for example, if a stocktake reveals totals which differ from QuickBooks' totals).

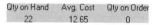

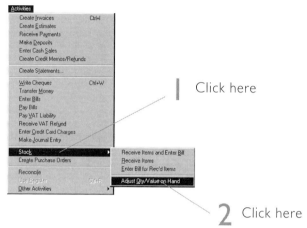

| Click here

2 Click here

Re step 6 – to adjust the stock item total upwards, type in a positive number e.g.:   4

To adjust the total downwards, enter a negative number e.g.:   -6

Now carry out steps 3 and 4 below. Perform step 5 or 6. Finally, carry out step 7:

3 Type in the effective date

4 Click here; select an expense account

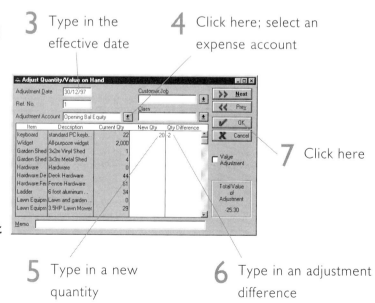

After step 7, the manual adjustment is entered into your stock register (see page 122).

7 Click here

5 Type in a new quantity

6 Type in an adjustment difference

The stock register

Like all QuickBooks accounts, the Stock Asset account has a register. You can use this to view – and inspect – each item sold, purchased or amended.

Launching the stock register
First, launch your Chart of Accounts (see page 67 for how to do this). Now do the following:

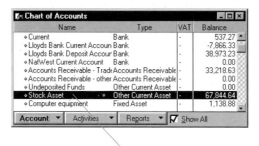

Double-click here

HANDY TIP

To view an item, click it. Then press Ctrl+E. The underlying window (e.g. the Create Invoices window) launches.
Click OK when you've finished using it.

The Stock Asset register launches:

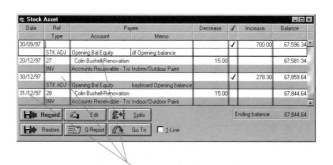

HANDY TIP

See pages 82–83 for more information on using account registers.

Individual sales, purchases or adjustments

To close the register when you've finished using it, press Esc. Press Esc again to close your Chart of Accounts.

VAT

Chapter Six

In this chapter, you'll discover how to track VAT in QuickBooks UK. You'll learn about the VAT Control account, a special liability account which QuickBooks uses to monitor your output and input tax. You'll set up your QuickBooks company for VAT tracking, and establish a VAT opening balance. You'll also make manual VAT adjustments to correct errors, and use three special reports to view your VAT situation graphically. Finally, you'll pay VAT and enter refunds.

Covers

Tracking VAT – an overview

Below are two definitions which are crucial to QuickBooks UK's implementation of VAT tracking:

Output tax

This book is not a manual on the implementation of VAT.

If you need more detailed help with VAT, consult your local HM Customs and Excise office.

VAT is a consumer-directed tax on the sale and purchase of goods. Businesses which are VAT-registered (the threshold is currently in the region of £47,000) are obliged to charge VAT to their customers on the invoices they submit to them. This is known as output tax.

Input tax

By the same token, when third-party goods or services are purchased, registered businesses may well – in turn – be charged VAT. This is known as input tax. Input tax is normally recoverable.

Expressed rather simplistically, the following formulas apply:

— the VAT you charge your customers minus the VAT you've incurred equals what you have to pay HM Customs and Excise (if the result is a positive number)

— the VAT you've incurred minus the VAT you charge your customers equals what HM Customs and Excise have to refund to you (if the result is a positive number)

To make it as easy as possible to track VAT, QuickBooks UK :

1. automatically creates (when you create your company – see Chapter Two – and if you opt for VAT tracking) a special VAT account known as VAT Control. When you raise invoices or pay bills, QuickBooks excerpts the relevant VAT amounts and inserts them in your VAT Control account

2. produces special reports which make the completion of VAT returns much easier (see pages 130–132 for more information)

More on the VAT Control account

This is a unique QuickBooks liability account which exists specifically to record:

- output VAT to clients

- input VAT on costs

Output VAT is recorded in a column called 'Increase', input VAT in a column called 'Decrease':

The Increase column

The Decrease column

REMEMBER

If you run more than one business and need to track VAT separately, you must set up a separate QuickBooks company for each.

If you're VAT-registered, you can use QuickBooks UK to keep track of input and output tax, easily and conveniently. Before you can do this, however, you have to

1.   prepare for VAT the company you created in the EasyStep Interview (see pages 126–127).

2.   enter an opening balance in your VAT Control account (see page 128).

Setting up your company for VAT

During the EasyStep Interview (Chapter Two, pages 38–39), you answered a series of questions about whether your company tracked VAT, and – if so – on what basis. If you do track VAT, the necessary information includes:

- the name of your VAT agency, and your Registration ID

- details of your reporting period

- the reporting basis

- details of whether you want to enter invoices and cash sales exclusive, or inclusive, of VAT.

If you want, you can change the VAT settings at any time. Even if you don't want to change any of the settings you implemented in the Interview, it's a good idea to verify that they *are* correct now.

REMEMBER

To qualify for the Cash accounting scheme, a business' annual turnover must be under £350,000.

Reporting bases

QuickBooks recognises two ways to pay VAT (known as VAT schemes):

HANDY TIP

The Cash accounting scheme has its drawbacks, too: for instance, businesses have to wait longer before reclaiming VAT charged by suppliers.

Accrual	This is the standard method. The day on which goods are despatched to a customer (or services completed) is the day from which the associated VAT is due (whether or not the bill is paid).
Cash accounting	The date on which a bill is sent out is ignored. Instead, the VAT is only due when the bill is paid.

Preparing for VAT use

Pull down the File menu and carry out the following steps:

Click here

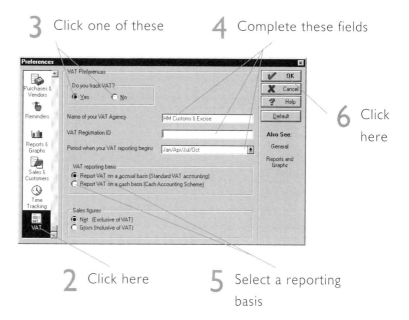

3 Click one of these

4 Complete these fields

6 Click here

2 Click here

5 Select a reporting basis

Setting up a VAT opening balance

You need to ensure your VAT Control account has the appropriate opening balance.

Bear in mind that – effective from your Start date (see Chapter Two, page 40 for more information on how to set Start dates) – what you owe is the net result of taking into account the following factors:

1. payments you've received from customers and what they owe you

2. payments you've made and what you owe vendors

As a result of the above, the best – and, in the long term, the easiest – way to ensure the VAT Control account has the correct opening balance is to enter, in the normal way (but see the Handy Tip on the left), *all* historical (i.e. retrospective) transactions relating to your Start date's VAT quarter. The benefits conferred by entering historical transactions include:

- your accounts will balance accurately

- you have exact records of monies you owe and are owed

- reports you generate (see Chapter Ten) are fully up to date

- up-to-date profit and loss statements (see Chapter Ten)

When you enter historical transactions, QuickBooks UK ensures that all the necessary VAT information is entered automatically into your VAT Control account, including the figures for 1 and 2 above.

HANDY TIP

Bear the following in mind when you enter historical transactions:

- **enter past current or bank account transactions last (and ensure QuickBooks hasn't already entered them)**
- **enter accounts receivable transactions in the following order:** invoices – cash sales – returns – payments – deposits
- **enter accounts payable transactions in the following order:** bills – vendor credits –payments

Manual VAT adjustments

There are times when you may need to make manual adjustments to your VAT Control account. For example, you may have to correct a shortfall in a payment, or a mistake on your return.

Implementing an adjustment

Launch your Chart of Accounts. (For how to do this, see page 67.) Now do the following:

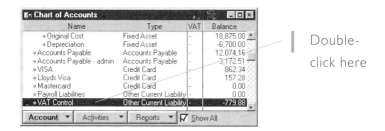

| Double-click here

Now carry out step 2 below. Perform step 3 or 4, depending on the type of adjustment. Finally, carry out step 5:

2 Enter a date for the adjustment

4 Enter an amount for *deductible* VAT

Before carrying out steps 2–5, choose a new (blank) transaction at the end of the register. (Press Ctrl+End to reach this location.)

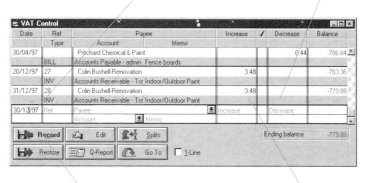

5 Click here

3 Enter an amount for *payable* VAT

VAT reports

QuickBooks UK lets you view your VAT status as a report. There are three VAT report types:

Details of VAT reports

VAT Summary   supplies brief details of VAT amounts, organised by VAT code and relative to a specified accounting period

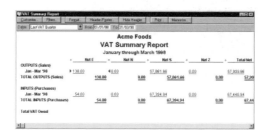

VAT Summary report

VAT Detail   an expanded version of the VAT Summary report. Supplies very comprehensive details of individual VAT amounts, organised by category (output or input) and date. As with VAT Summary, can be targeted at a specific period

The third VAT report type is 'VAT 100'. Use this to complete your VAT 100 return (see page 132).

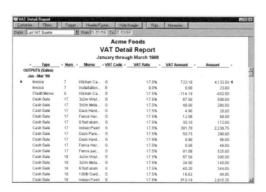

VAT Detail report

...contd

Generating a VAT report

Pull down the Reports menu and do the following:

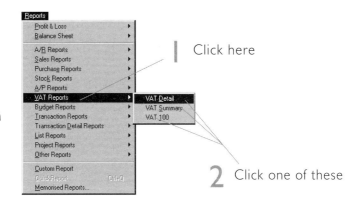

Click here

For more help with reports in general, see Chapter Ten.

2 Click one of these

Specifying the report period

In any of the VAT reports, carry out step 3 or 4 below:

3 Click here; select a preset period

After step 4, click anywhere outside the From and To fields to have QuickBooks UK recreate the graph.

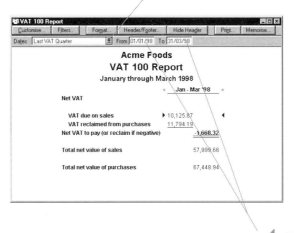

4 Type in start and end dates

Using VAT 100 reports

Five totals on the VAT 100 report have to be inserted into your VAT 100 return form when you complete it. Follow the instructions below:

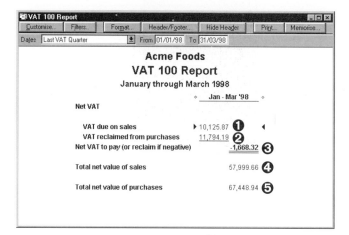

See below for where to insert data in the report form

❶ enter this figure into the 'VAT due in this period on sales and other outputs' box

❷ enter this figure into the 'VAT reclaimed in this period on purchases and other inputs...' box

❸ enter this figure into the 'Net VAT to be paid to Customs or reclaimed by you...' box

❹ enter this figure into the 'Total value of sales and all other outputs excluding any VAT...' box

❺ enter this figure into the 'Total value of purchases and all other inputs excluding any VAT...' box

Paying your VAT

Follow the procedures below to pay money you owe to HM Customs & Excise.

Pull down the Activities menu and do the following:

Click here

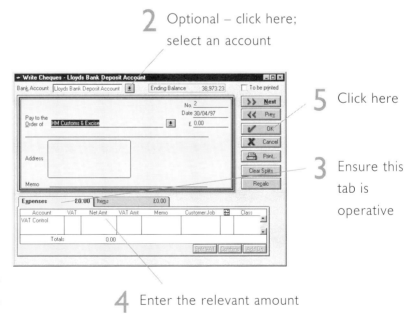

2 Optional – click here; select an account

5 Click here

3 Ensure this tab is operative

4 Enter the relevant amount

REMEMBER

The amount you enter in step 4 appears as a decrease in your VAT Control account.

REMEMBER

See Chapter Nine for more information on how to produce cheques.

Entering VAT refunds

Follow the procedures below to enter refunds you receive from HM Customs & Excise.

Pull down the Activities menu and do the following:

| Click here

The amount you enter in step 3 appears as an increase in your VAT Control account.

2 Optional – click here; select an account

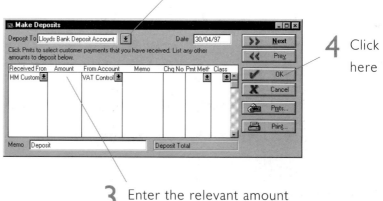

4 Click here

3 Enter the relevant amount

Accounts receivable

This chapter shows you how to use the QuickBooks accounts receivable feature. You'll use the A/R register to amend existing transactions and track linked transactions; additionally, you'll adjust customer opening balances in the customer register, and record returned cheques. Finally, you'll enter invoice payments, and also overpayments, down payments and advance payments.

Chapter Seven

Covers

The A/R register – an overview

The Interview *may* create more than one A/R account.

Accounts receivable (otherwise known as A/R) is an accounting term which refers to balances due from debtors – in other words, money owed on invoices which have not yet been paid. QuickBooks UK monitors accounts receivable in a single account automatically created in your Chart of Accounts in the course of the EasyStep Interview (see Chapter Two).

You can use QuickBooks accounts receivable to:

- amend existing transactions

- amend the opening balances for specific customers

- have QuickBooks UK locate and display transactions which are linked to a specific transaction (this is called viewing a 'transaction history')

You can also use a specific form to enter transactions which have an *indirect* effect on your accounts receivable account. You can enter:

To record bounced cheques, carry out stage 1 below, and then stage 2 in the Handy Tip on page 137:
1. Create a new Other Charge item called 'Bad Cheque'. (To create items, perform the relevant steps on pages 113–114, but amend them in line with refinements listed here.) Apply this to your current account; do not amend the Amount or % field.

- invoice payments

- overpayments

- down payments

- advance payments

You interact *directly* with the accounts receivable account via a standard QuickBooks register:

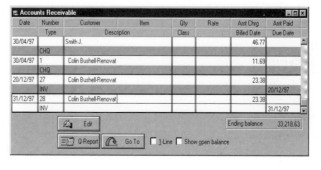

The accounts receivable register

Launching the A/R register

HANDY TIP

To record bounced cheques, carry out stage 1 on page 136, then stage 2:

2. Click Create Invoices in the Activities menu. Apply a customer in the Customer:Job field. Amend the Tax Date entry to the date your bank reversed the deposit. Type in the cheque amount (inc. any charges) in the Amount field. In the Item field, select Bad Cheque. In the Terms field, click Due on receipt. (Optional – in the Memo field, insert a reference to the invoice(s) the bounced cheque related to.)

To print the invoice, click Print. In the message, click No. Now complete the Print One Invoice dialog. Click OK.

Back in the Create Invoices window, click OK.

To launch an accounts receivable register, pull down the Lists menu and do the following:

Click here

2 Double-click an accounts receivable account

The customer register

The customer register is a special register which provides accounts receivable information from the perspective of individual customers.

Launching the customer register

Pull down the Activities menu and do the following:

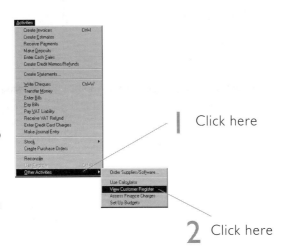

Click '1-Line' in the register to have every transaction appear on a single line (more are therefore visible).

Click here

1

Click here

2

See below for a list of fields in the accounts receivable register and their functions:

Click here; select a customer

3

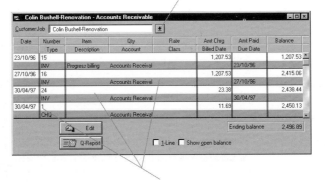

Individual transactions

(e.g. invoices or cheques)

Type   shows the transaction type

Amt Chrge   shows invoice amounts

Amt Paid   shows payment amounts

Editing A/R transactions

If you have trouble locating a transaction in a register, click here:

The Go To dialog launches. Click the arrow to the right of the Which Field box; select a field you want to search through. In the Search For box, type in text and/or a number which identifies the transaction you want to locate. Click Prev to have QuickBooks search backwards, or Next to search forwards.

QuickBooks finds the first matching transaction. Press Esc to close the Go To dialog when you've finished with it.

In either of the following:

• the accounts receivable register

• the customer register

you can amend existing transactions. Carry out steps 1–2 below:

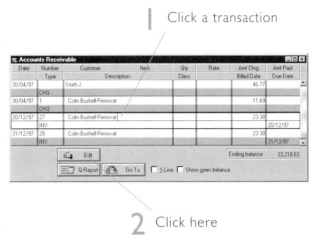

Click a transaction

2 Click here

QuickBooks reopens the transaction in its original form. Amend this in the usual way, then carry out step 3 below:

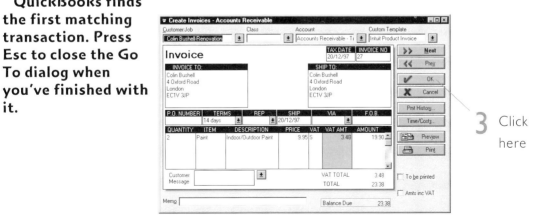

3 Click here

Adjusting A/R opening balances

REMEMBER

The process of entering *all* **historical transactions (see page 128) ensures that your A/R account's opening balance is the sum of customer balances.**

This also applies to A/P (accounts payable) accounts (see Chapter Nine). However, it's necessary to enter some opening balances manually when you first use or create accounts. Use the following guidelines for other account types (as at your Start date):

Bank   the amount in your bank

Asset   the value of the asset

Credit card what you owe

Liability   the extent of your liability

You can amend accounts receivable balances in the following way.

Pull down the Lists menu and do the following:

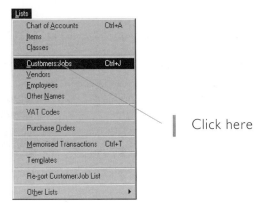

Click here

2 Select a customer

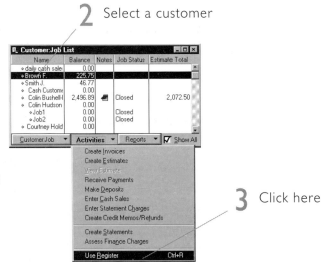

3 Click here

Now complete steps 4–7 on page 141.

...contd

Carry out the additional steps below:

4 Click the opening
balance transaction

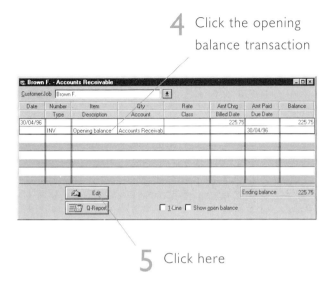

5 Click here

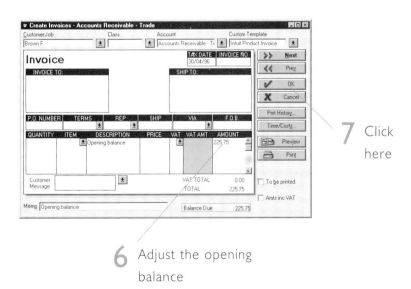

7 Click
here

6 Adjust the opening
balance

Transaction histories

From within either of the following:

* the A/R register

* the window which launches when you carry out steps 1–2 on page 139

HANDY TIP **You can also view transaction histories in bank account registers.**

you can view transactions which are associated with a pre-selected transaction (for example, payments which were made in response to an originating invoice). QuickBooks UK calls this process looking up a 'transaction history'.

Launching a transaction history

Click the relevant transaction in the A/R register. (Optionally, you can also press Ctrl+R to launch the appropriate form.) Then pull down the Edit menu and do the following:

HANDY TIP **Click the Edit button if you need to edit the information contained in the originally specified transaction.**
  Make the necessary changes, then click OK.

Click here

HANDY TIP **Click the Go To button if you need to edit the information contained in the selected linked transaction.**
  Make the necessary changes, then click OK.

Details of the specified transaction

2 Click here

A linked transaction (here, the originating invoice)

Entering invoice payments

The way QuickBooks UK records accounts receivable data in a single, overall account pays dividends when you receive and record invoice payments. For example, you can view a customer's payment history and a list of overdue invoices; this information is pulled from the underlying A/R account.

 Any credits resulting from overpayments or credit memos are shown in the Existing Credits section of the Receive Payments window:

Credits appear here

Entering invoice payments

Pull down the Activities menu and carry out the following steps:

Click here

 Re step 3 – after you enter the payment amount, QuickBooks may pre-select an unpaid invoice at the base of the window.

2 Click here; select a customer/job

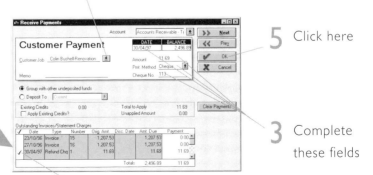

5 Click here

3 Complete these fields

 Unpaid invoices are shown here:

4 If necessary, click the relevant invoice (a ✔ appears to the left)

Handling overpayments

HANDY TIP

To enter a down or advance payment, carry out steps 1–3 on page 143, *but* omit step 4. The payment is shown in this field:

Unapplied Amount   100.00

Perform step 5. When you reopen the Receive Payments window and select the relevant customer, the payment appears as a credit in the Existing Credits field. When you've generated the appropriate invoice, simply select it here: and apply the credit to it in the normal way.

QuickBooks UK adopts a somewhat modified payment procedure when you're entering:

• overpayments

• down payments

• advance payments

Entering overpayments

Follow steps 1–4 on page 143; as part of step 3, enter the overpayment:

The overpayment...

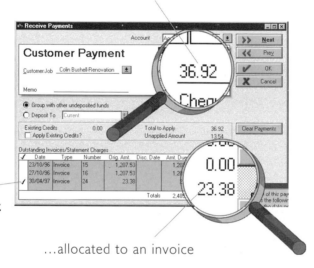

...allocated to an invoice

Finally, follow step 5 on page 143.

If you only applied the overpayment to one invoice (in spite of the fact that there were additional overdue invoices), and part of the overpayment is therefore still outstanding, a special message appears. Do the following:

REMEMBER

After step 1, generate the relevant credit memo (see pages 97–98 for how to do this).

Click here

Purchase orders

This chapter shows you how to buy stock with purchase orders. You'll view a dedicated purchase order report; turn on QuickBooks' purchase order feature (if you didn't do this in the EasyStep Interview); generate and print new purchase orders; and, in the process, customise your own purchase order format. Finally, you'll amend existing purchase orders; receive stock against them; and mark individual stock items as closed.

Covers

Chapter Eight

Purchase orders – an overview

When you place orders for items (subject to conditions 1 and 2 below), you should use the QuickBooks purchase order (PO) feature. Using purchase orders:

- contributes very effectively to the stock monitoring process

- provides live details – on request – of which items are on order

Use purchase orders when you're ordering stock which is subject to both of the following conditions:

1. you'll pay for it later

2. you'll receive it later

A special account...

When you generate your first purchase order, QuickBooks UK automatically creates a new account called Purchase Orders. This (normally to be found as the last account in your Chart of Accounts) tracks all purchase orders as a report, showing all relevant details.

Purchase orders whose stock items have not yet been delivered (called open purchase orders) are listed in the Purchase Orders list.
  See page 153 for how to identify, view and edit outstanding purchase orders.

To close the Purchase Orders account report, simply press Esc.
  See Chapter Ten for more information on reports.

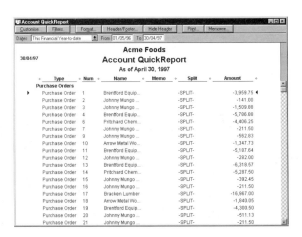

The result of double-clicking the Purchase Orders account in your Chart of Accounts

...contd

In the EasyStep Interview, you will have decided whether or not to track stock. (See page 35 for more information.) You must have opted for stock tracking to be able to use purchase orders. Alternatively, you can do so now.

To turn off purchase order/ stock tracking, simply follows steps 1–4 again.

Turning on the PO (stock tracking) feature

Pull down the File menu and do the following:

Click here

Purchase orders are primarily intended to be used if you keep stock. However, you can still use them even if you don't...

3 Click here

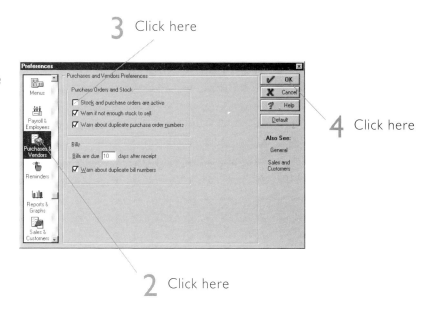

4 Click here

2 Click here

Creating POs – initial steps

You can use purchase orders to order:

- stock items

- services (or other non-stock items)

You generate purchase orders via the Create Purchase Orders window. You can launch this in two ways:

When you order stock items, QuickBooks UK updates your stock records automatically.
Note, however, that this sort of updating doesn't apply to non-stock items.

The menu route

Pull down the Activities menu and do the following:

Click here

The Navigator route

Carry out the following steps:

Click here

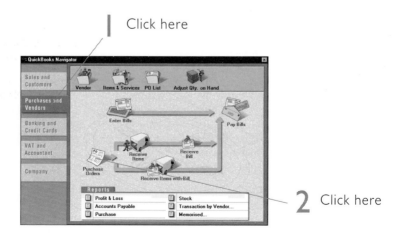

2 Click here

Creating POs – stage 1

Now complete the Create Purchase Orders window. There are three stages to this process. In the first, you complete the customer section of the window.

 HANDY TIP

Re step 1 – selecting a vendor inserts the associated address into the Vendor field.

Perform steps 1–3 below:

Click here; select a vendor

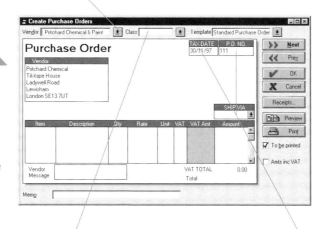

 HANDY TIP

To change the purchase order format, click the arrow to the right of the Template field; in the box, select a new format.

Selecting a new format may vary, to some extent, the fields contained in the Create Purchase Orders window.

2 Optional – click here; select a class

3 Optional – change the date or purchase order no.

More help with stage 1 (1)

Step 1 above

QuickBooks UK maintains a list of vendors; completing this field is mandatory. If none of the existing vendors are applicable, select <Add New> in the list. Now carry out steps 1–3 on page 150.

...contd

Complete steps 1–3 to create a new vendor:

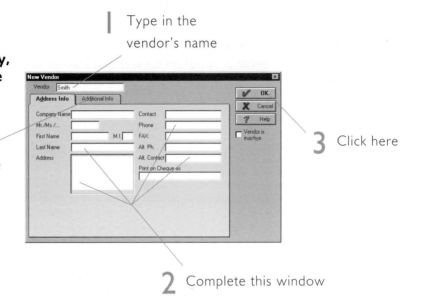

HANDY TIP

If necessary, complete the remainder of this dialog.

Click this tab: then complete the additional fields. **Finally, carry out step 3.**

Type in the vendor's name

3 Click here

2 Complete this window

More help with stage 1 (2)

Step 2 on page 149

This field is inoperative if – in the course of the EasyStep Interview – you did not opt to use QuickBooks classes. If none of the existing classes are applicable, select <Add New> in the list. Now carry out steps A–B below:

REMEMBER

You can create subclasses, too.

Follow step A to name the new subclass. Click here: **Now click here:** **In the list, select a host class. Lastly, perform step B.**

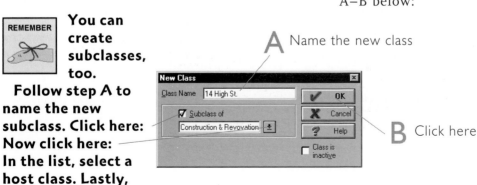

A Name the new class

B Click here

Creating POs – stage 2

In stage 2 in the purchase order completion process, you enter item information.

Perform steps 1–4 below:

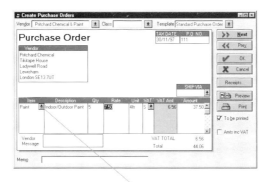

Click here; select an item in the list

More help with stage 2

Step 1 above

If none of the existing items are applicable, select <Add New> in the list. Now carry out steps 2–4 below:

2 Click here; select an item type (normally, Stock Part)

HANDY TIP

Re step 3 – the fields within this dialog depend on the item type chosen in step 1. Complete them as appropriate.

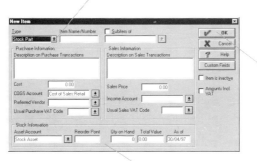

4 Click here

3 Complete the rest of the dialog

Creating POs – stage 3

HANDY TIP

To create your own purchase order format, click the arrow to the right of the Template field; in the box, select Customise.

In the Select a template field in the Customise Template dialog, click Custom Purchase Order. Click Edit. Work through the tabs in the Customise Purchase Order dialog, selecting and naming the fields you want to appear. Click OK.

Finally, back in the Create Purchase Orders window, click the arrow to the right of the Template field; in the box, select Custom Purchase Order. Complete the rest of the window (see pages 149–152 for how to do this).

In the third and final stage of the purchase order completion process, you enter sales information. Note, however, that carrying out steps 1–2 in the sales section of the Create Purchase Orders dialog is entirely optional.

Perform steps 1–2 below, as appropriate. Finally, perform step 3.

Click here; enter a message

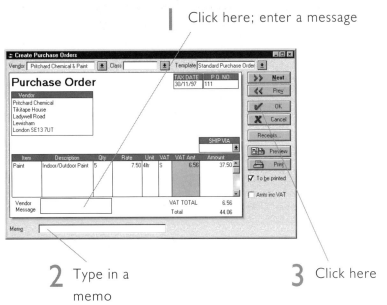

2 Type in a memo

3 Click here

More help with stage 3

Step 2 above

You can enter a one-off message (called a 'memo') here. Memos:

- do not appear on the printed versions of purchase orders

- do appear in other places where QuickBooks makes reference to purchase orders.

Editing purchase orders

You can amend existing purchase orders, if necessary.

HANDY TIP

To delete a purchase order, carry out step 1. Press Ctrl+D. In the message, click OK.

Pull down the Lists menu and click Purchase Orders. Now do the following:

Click a purchase order

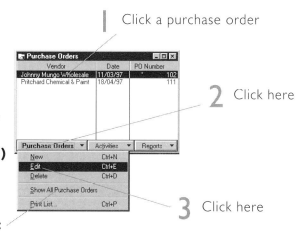

2 Click here

HANDY TIP

Here, only open (i.e. unfulfilled) purchase orders are shown. To view *all* orders, however, click here:

3 Click here

Perform the following steps:

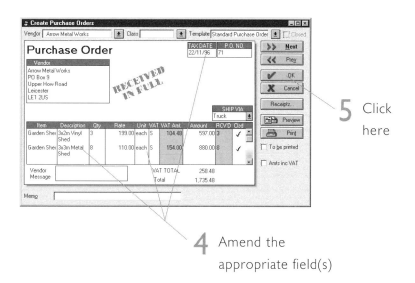

5 Click here

4 Amend the appropriate field(s)

Printing purchase orders

REMEMBER

If your purchase orders don't print with the correct alignment, click the Align button in the dialog below. Complete the dialogs which launch, following the on-screen instructions.

You can print purchase orders in two ways:

- singly, from within the Create Purchase Orders window

- in groups, from within a separate dialog

Printing purchase orders singly

Launch the Create Purchase Orders window in the normal way (see page 148 for how to do this). Click this button:

Now carry out the following steps, as appropriate:

REMEMBER

Re step 2 – choose 'Page-oriented' to print to laser or inkjet printers, or 'Continuous' to print to dot matrix printers.

REMEMBER

If you need to adjust your printer's internal settings, click this button:

Now complete the dialog(s) which launch, as appropriate. Finally, follow step 6 to begin printing.

2 Click here; select a printer type

1 Click here; select a printer in the list

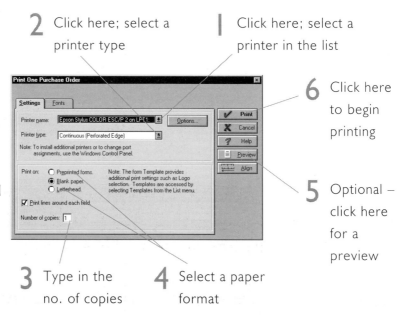

6 Click here to begin printing

5 Optional – click here for a preview

3 Type in the no. of copies

4 Select a paper format

Step 5 launches the Print Preview window; when you've finished using this, click this button to initiate printing directly:

...contd

Printing purchase orders in groups

Pull down the File menu and do the following:

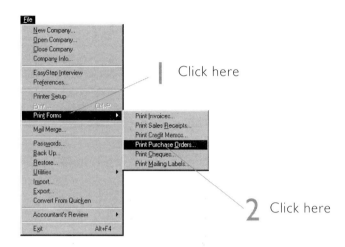

Click here

Ensure your printer is on-line and switched on (and that there is enough paper in it) before you begin printing.

REMEMBER

Click here

Now complete the following steps:

3 Click as many sales forms as you want to print (a ✔ appears against each)

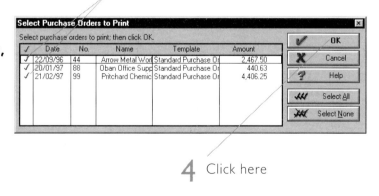

To list a purchase order in this dialog, first select this field:

HANDY TIP

in the Create Purchase Orders window *before* you follow the procedures here.

4 Click here

After step 4, QuickBooks launches an additional dialog – follow steps 1–6 on page 154.

Manual closures

QuickBooks UK automatically marks a purchase order as 'RECEIVED IN FULL' as soon as all its items have been received (and entered as such – see the Remember tip). However, there are circumstances when you may wish to mark *specific* items as closed (e.g. if they're no longer made, and cannot therefore be supplied).

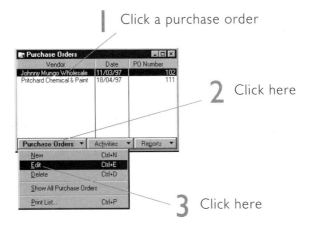

REMEMBER

See pages 117–119 for the procedures to adopt when you receive pre-ordered stock.

Closing items on purchase orders

Pull down the Lists menu and click Purchase Orders. Now carry out the following steps:

1 Click a purchase order

2 Click here

3 Click here

Perform the following steps:

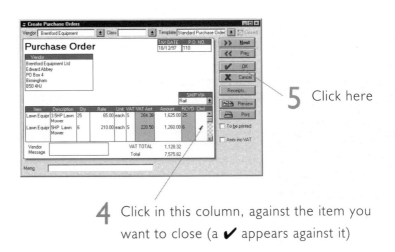

5 Click here

4 Click in this column, against the item you want to close (a ✔ appears against it)

Accounts payable

This chapter shows you how to use the QuickBooks accounts payable feature. You'll use the A/P register to amend existing transactions and track linked transactions; additionally, you'll adjust vendor opening balances. Finally, you'll enter and pay bills; print cheques; and have QuickBooks remind you when bills are due.

Chapter Nine

Covers

The A/P register – an overview

Accounts payable (otherwise known as A/P) is an accounting term which refers to a business's outstanding bills – in other words, money owed to creditors.

REMEMBER

Your Chart of Accounts *may* **contain more than one accounts payable account.**

QuickBooks UK monitors accounts payable in a single account (the Accounts Payable account) which is automatically created when you record your first bill.

You can use QuickBooks' accounts payable feature to:

• amend existing transactions

• amend the opening balances for specific vendors

• have QuickBooks UK locate and display transactions which are linked to a specific transaction (this is called viewing a 'transaction history')

When you enter/pay bills or print cheques, the results appear in the accounts payable register:

BEWARE

If you pay bills on receipt, you don't need to use the A/P bill entering and paying procedures described on pages 163–164. Instead, use the Write Cheques window to pay bills direct (see pages 166–167).

An accounts payable register

Payment transactions

Reminders
You can have QuickBooks remind you when a bill is due to be paid.

Launching the A/P register

To launch an accounts payable register, pull down the Lists menu and do the following:

Click here

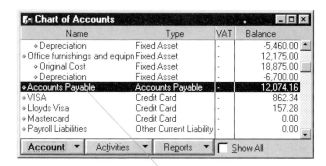

2 Double-click an accounts payable account

Editing A/P transactions

You can use the accounts payable register to amend existing transactions. Carry out steps 1–2 below:

Click a transaction

If you have trouble locating a transaction in a register, click here:

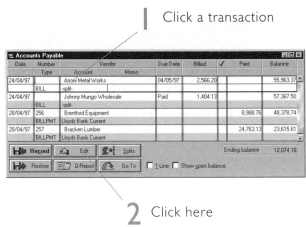

The Go To dialog launches. Click the arrow to the right of the Which Field box; select a field you want to search through. In the Search For box, type in text and/or a number which identifies the transaction you want to locate. Click Prev to have QuickBooks search backwards, or Next to search forwards.

QuickBooks finds the first matching transaction. Press Esc to close the Go To dialog when you've finished with it.

2 Click here

QuickBooks reopens the transaction in its original form. Amend this in the usual way (see page 163 for how to do this), then carry out step 3 below:

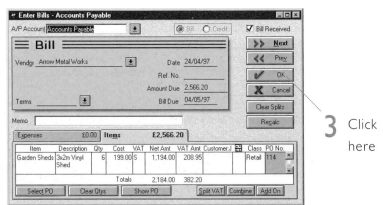

3 Click here

Adjusting A/P opening balances

You can amend accounts payable balances in the following way.

Amending a vendor's opening balance

Press Ctrl+A. Now do the following:

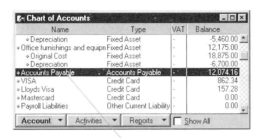

The process of entering *all* historical transactions (see page 128) ensures that your A/P account's opening balance is the sum of vendor balances.

1 Double-click an accounts payable account

2 Click the relevant opening balance transaction and amend the amount

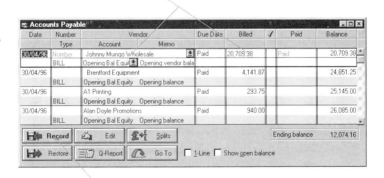

3 Click here

Transaction histories

From within either of the following:

- the A/P register

- the window which launches when you carry out steps 1–2 on page 160

You can also view transaction histories in bank account registers.

you can view transactions which are associated with a pre-selected transaction (for example, payments which were made in response to an originating bill). QuickBooks UK calls this process looking up a 'transaction history'.

Launching a transaction history

Click the relevant transaction in the A/P register. (Optionally, press Ctrl+R to launch the appropriate form.) Then pull down the Edit menu and do the following:

Click the Edit button if you need to edit the information contained in the originally specified transaction.
Make the necessary changes, then click OK.

Click here

Click the Go To button if you need to edit the information contained in the selected linked transaction.
Make the necessary changes, then click OK.

Details of the specified transaction

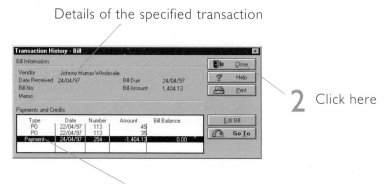

2 Click here

A linked transaction (here, the bill payment)

Entering bills

It's advisable to enter bills as soon as you receive them. This ensures that any cash-flow reports you generate are as up-to-date as possible.

Re step 2 – if open purchase orders are associated with the vendor you choose, a special message launches. If you want to receive against one of these, do the following:

Click here

In the Open Purchase Orders dialog, click the relevant purchase order. Click OK. Back in the Enter Bills window, perform step 3 but not 4 (QuickBooks completes this for you). Finally, carry out step 5.

You can use the QuickBooks accounts payable feature to:

1. record bills in the Enter Bills window

2. pay them later in the Pay Bills window

Recording a bill

Pull down the Activities menu and do the following:

Click here

2 Click here; select a vendor

3 Complete these fields, as appropriate

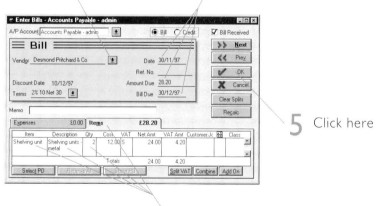

5 Click here

4 Click this tab, then complete the item detail fields

Bill payment

You can use the Pay Bills window to:

You can delete a bill or payment. Within any A/P register, click the transaction. Press Ctrl+D. In the message which launches, click OK. (Deleting paid bills raises a credit with the associated vendor; deleting payments gives the associated bill an unpaid balance.)

1.   pay one or more bills

2.   (additionally) print out the relevant cheque

Paying bills

Pull down the Activities menu and do the following:

Click here

2 Enter a
   payment date

3 Optional – enter a date up to
   which bills are to be displayed

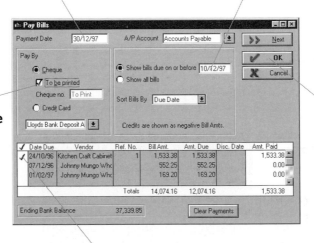

Ensure this is ticked: to have the relevant cheque printed. (See page 165 for how to do this.)

5 Click here

4 Click one or more bills

Drawing cheques

HANDY TIP

To draw a cheque directly from a bank account (i.e. without recourse to the Enter Bills and Pay Bills windows), see pages 166–167.

To produce a cheque to pay a bill, follow steps 1–5 on page 164, then do the following:

Printing cheques to pay bills

Pull down the File menu and do the following:

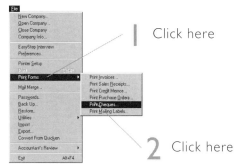

1 Click here

2 Click here

REMEMBER

Re step 6 – choose Page-oriented to print to laser or inkjet printers, or Continuous to print to dot matrix printers.

4 Click here

3 Click a cheque

REMEMBER

If you need to adjust your printer's internal settings, click this button:

6 Click here; select a printer type

5 Click here; select a printer in the list

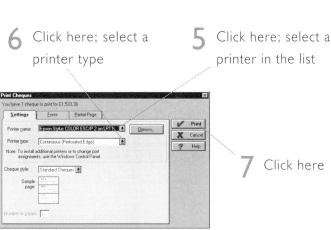

7 Click here

Now complete the dialog(s) which launch, as appropriate. Finally, follow step 7 to begin printing.

...contd

You can generate cheques independently via the Write Cheques window.

Printing standalone cheques

Pull down the Activities menu and do the following:

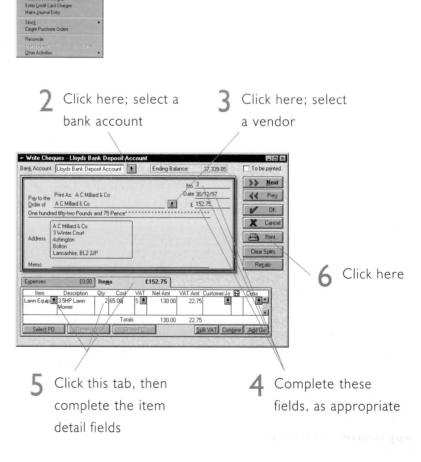

| Click here

HANDY TIP

Re step 3 – if open purchase orders are associated with the vendor you choose, a special message launches. If you want to receive against one of these, do the following:

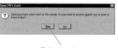

Click here

In the Open Purchase Orders dialog, click the relevant purchase order(s); a ✔ appears to the left. Click OK. Back in the Write Cheques window, complete step 4 but ignore 5 (QuickBooks completes this for you). Finally, carry out step 6.

2 Click here; select a bank account

3 Click here; select a vendor

6 Click here

5 Click this tab, then complete the item detail fields

4 Complete these fields, as appropriate

...contd

REMEMBER

To delete a cheque, select it in its current account register. Press Ctrl+D. In the message, click OK. (Deleting cheques removes the transaction permanently.)

To void a cheque, select it in its current account register. Pull down the Edit menu and click Void Cheque; QuickBooks resets the cheque amount to zero.

REMEMBER

If you need to adjust your printer's internal settings, click this button:

⌐ Options... ¬

Now complete the dialog(s) which launch, as appropriate. Finally, follow step 5 to begin printing.

Now carry out the following additional steps:

Type in the number of the cheque you want to print

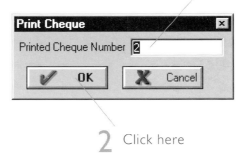

2 Click here

4 Click here; select a printer type

3 Click here; select a printer in the list

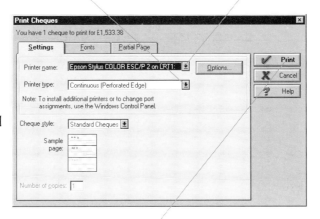

5 Click here

Bill reminders

You can have QuickBooks remind you when bills are due to be paid.

 You can have a summary of bills displayed, or a detailed list. (See step 3 – and the 'Viewing the Reminders window' heading – below.)

Setting bill reminder preferences
Pull down the File menu and do the following:

Click here

 You can also use this dialog to set other reminder preferences. For example, you can have QuickBooks prompt you to reorder stock...

2 Click here

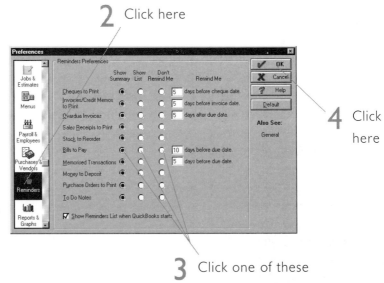

4 Click here

3 Click one of these

 Re step 3 – if you select Show Summary or Show List, do the following:

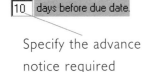

Specify the advance notice required

Viewing the Reminders window
By default, a list of reminders displays when you start QuickBooks UK. To view this at will, however, pull down the Lists menu and click Other Lists > Reminders. To close the list, press Esc.

Reports and graphs

This chapter shows you how to use QuickBooks UK's reports and graphs to achieve a rapid and detailed snapshot of your company's financial situation. You'll create and customise reports and graphs, then you'll print them out.

Covers

Chapter Ten

Reports and graphs – an overview

QuickBooks UK makes managing your company's finances easy. However, it's also vital to be able to take an overview of them. You can do this in two ways:

- verbally, by generating reports

- visually, by generating graphs

QuickBooks has over 60 report formats which you can use to achieve a detailed written evaluation of your company's finances. Utilise its graphing capability to make a similar kind of evaluation *instantly*. Better still, use both reports and graphs for a comprehensive picture of how your finances are progressing.

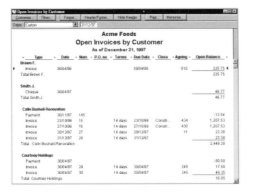

An A/R Open Invoices report

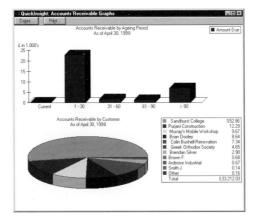

An A/R graph

Report types

The following are among the overall report types you can use in QuickBooks UK:

Profit and loss	e.g. Standard (summarises income/expenses) and By Class (income/expenses organised by classes/subclasses)
Balance sheet	e.g. Standard (displays balances for balance sheet accounts)
A/R	e.g. Open Invoices (displays details of unpaid invoices)
Sales	includes reports which display sales by item or customer, and pending sales
Purchase	includes reports which display purchases by item or vendor, and outstanding purchase orders
Stock	includes reports which display the status of stock items by item or vendor
A/P	e.g. Unpaid Bills Detail (displays outstanding bills), and reports which list the ageing status of unpaid bills
VAT	see pages 130–132
List	numerous miscellaneous reports (e.g. Customer Phone – displays customers and their phone numbers)
Other	further miscellaneous reports (e.g. Cash Flow Forecast – projects income etc.)

Generating reports

You can have QuickBooks create reports in any of three ways:

The menu route
Pull down the Reports menu and do the following:

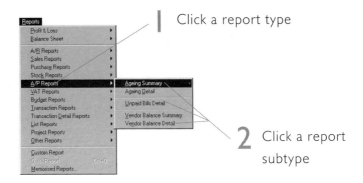

Click a report type

2 Click a report subtype

The Navigator route
Carry out the following steps:

Click one of these

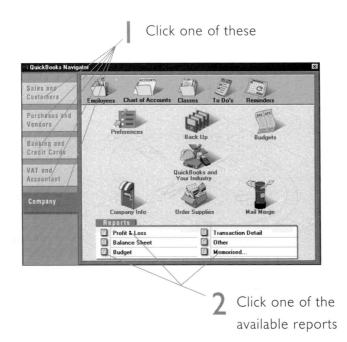

2 Click one of the available reports

...contd

QuickReport

You can also use a third method to create a report: QuickReport.

Within any list, register or form, do the following:

Re step 1 – here, we happen to be selecting a customer in the Create Invoices window. We could just as easily have selected a stock item in the Item List window, an account in the Chart of Accounts or a transaction in a register...

1 Select the name of the item or customer/ vendor you want information on.

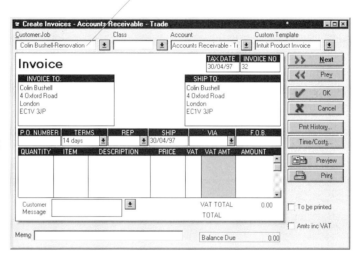

2 Now press Ctrl+Q.

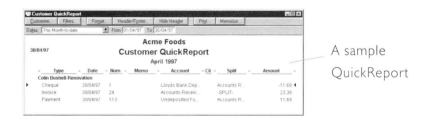

A sample QuickReport

3 Press Esc when you've finished using the QuickReport.

Customising reports

You can specify the way individual reports display.

REMEMBER

The fields in the lower section of the button bar vary according to the report type.

Customising reports

Refer to the button bar at the head of any report and do the following:

| Click here

Now carry out steps 2–4, as appropriate. Finally, perform step 5:

HANDY TIP

To apply new font details to a report,
click this button:

Format...

in the button bar. In the **Change Font For** field in the **Format Report** dialog, select a report element. Click the **Change Font** button. In the new dialog, make the necessary changes. Click OK. Back in the Format Report dialog, click OK.

2 Type in report start and end dates

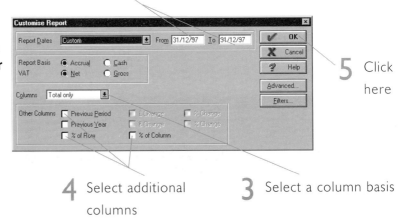

5 Click here

4 Select additional columns

3 Select a column basis

Generating graphs

It's sometimes useful to 'hide' one or more elements in a graph (this makes more room for the elements which remain).

Hold down one Shift key as you click a bar in a bar chart or a slice in a pie chart.

To restore hidden elements, recreate the graph.

QuickBooks graphs help you:

- compare income/expense

- view accounts receivable and accounts payable data

- compare assets/liabilities and view outstanding debts

- view sales figures

Creating a graph

Pull down the Graphs menu and do the following:

Click a graph type

To view the value associated with a graph element, right-click over it and hold down the mouse button:

Release the mouse button when you've finished.

This is the result:

Graph button bar

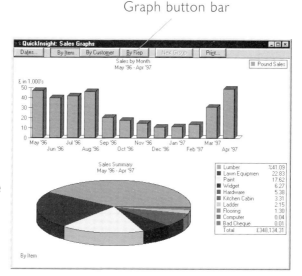

A Sales graph

Customising graphs

The fields in the graph button bar vary according to the graph type.

You can specify the way individual graphs display.

Customising graphs

Refer to the button bar at the head of any graph. Carry out step 1 (in the case of Income & Expenses and Sales graphs only) to specify how the data is organised. Perform steps 2–4 to apply a new date range.

By default, most graphs display data relating to the current financial year. To change this, follow steps 2–4.

1 Specify a graph basis

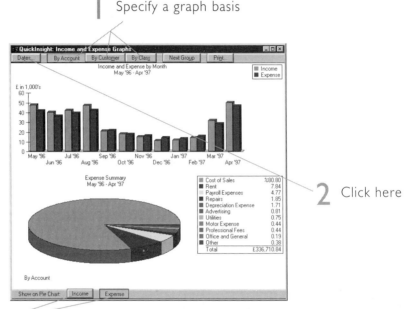

2 Click here

Most graphs contain a bar graph and a pie chart.

To customise the pie chart, click one of these fields: (this only applies to Income & Expense graphs).

3 Type in graph start and end dates

4 Click here

QuickZoom

In both reports and graphs, you can use a special feature called QuickZoom to obtain more information on selected components.

Using QuickZoom in reports

Move the mouse pointer over an amount:

When you move the mouse pointer over a valid report or graph item, it changes to:

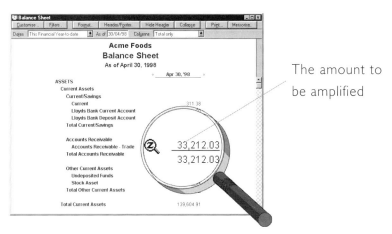

The amount to be amplified

Whether you use QuickZoom in a report or a graph, press Esc to close the QuickZoom window when you've finished with it.

Now double-click to produce a detailed breakdown.

Using QuickZoom in graphs

Move the mouse pointer over the item you need more information on:

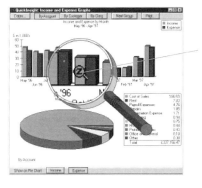

The item to be amplified

Now double-click to produce a detailed visual breakdown of the selected item.

Printing reports/graphs

See page 69 for a definition of the two types of orientation: Portrait and Landscape.

To print a report or graph, click the Print button in the button bar. Now do the following:

To print a report...

Carry out steps 1–4, as appropriate. Finally, perform step 5:

Click here; select a printer in the list

Re step 4 – you can initiate printing directly from within the Print Preview window. Simply click the Print button.

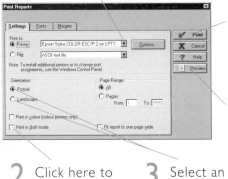

5 Click here to begin printing

4 Optional – click here for a preview

2 Click here to print in draft

3 Select an orientation

If you need to adjust your printer's internal settings, click this button:

Now complete the dialog(s) which launch, as appropriate. Finally, follow step 5 (above) or 3 (on the right) to begin printing.

To print a graph...

Carry out steps 1–2, as appropriate. Finally, perform step 3:

Click here; select a printer in the list

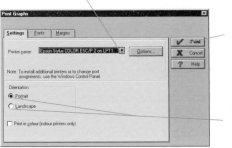

3 Click here to begin printing

2 Select an orientation

Reconciliation

Use this chapter to learn how to 'reconcile' (harmonise) your bank accounts with your statements. You'll use various techniques to compare deposits and withdrawals against statement entries, and isolate any discrepancies. Once located, inconsistencies can be adjusted easily and conveniently, or – if small – written off. Finally, you'll print out a reconciliation report.

Chapter Eleven

Covers

Reconciliation – an overview

The following QuickBooks account types have to be 'reconciled' against records kept by your bank:

- current accounts

- credit card accounts

- savings accounts

In essence, reconciliation simply involves verifying that transactions in your account match those in your statement.

In rather more detail, reconciliation is the process of:

 You control how accurate the reconciliation process is. For example, you don't *have* to account for every penny (but you can if you want to).

1. transposing bank statement information (e.g. bank charges and interest payments) into the corresponding QuickBooks account

2. comparing the statement with the account and marking as 'cleared' those transactions which are identical in both

3. totalling the number of deposit and withdrawal items in both the statement and account, and making sure the two totals tally

4. resolving any instances where the statement and account *don't* tally

Initial reconciliation

Normally, reconciliation is straightforward. However, when you reconcile an account for the first time, the situation can become rather more complex. This is because the initial setting up of an account involves inserting, as the opening balance, the balance on your latest statement.

This is fine provided that there were no outstanding withdrawals or deposits at the time. See page 181 for more information on initial reconciliation.

Initial balancing

To balance any of the account types listed on the previous page, follow the procedures set out in this chapter. However, there are certain special features you have to bear in mind if you're reconciling an account for the first time.

Balancing an account for the first time

You'll need to perform the following. Note, however, that stage 1 below applies to *any* account; it's just that, for initial reconciliations, the process will very probably take longer.

If you carry out step 2 on page 184 when the Difference field is 0.00, reconciliation is complete. A message launches. Do the following to print out a reconciliation report:

B Click here

A Click one of these

Complete the Print Lists dialog. Click OK.

1. enter, via the appropriate register, all transactions which:

    — haven't yet cleared

    — did not appear on earlier statements

    In practice, this shouldn't cause any problems because – as an inherent component of the reconciliation process – you can enter these transactions on-the-fly.

2. adjust the account's opening balance so that it equates to the figure which was in your account when you began using QuickBooks UK.

    You can do this by allowing QuickBooks to make its own adjustment at the end of the first reconciliation process

See pages 182–183 and 185 for how to carry out stage 1.

See the Handy Tip on page 184 for how to carry out stage 2.

Preparing to reconcile

You can start the reconciliation process in two ways:

The menu route

Pull down the Activities menu and do the following:

Click here

The Navigator route

Carry out the following steps:

Click here

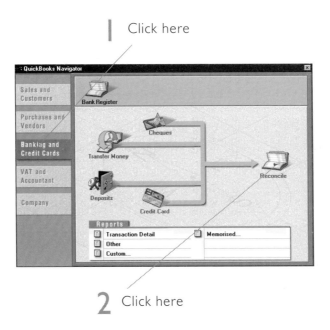

2 Click here

Reconciling an account

After following one of the procedures on page 182, do the following.

After following one of the procedures on page 182, do the following.

REMEMBER

After step 1, and before you carry out steps 2–4, do the following.

Compare the amount QuickBooks shows in the Opening Balance field: with your statement's opening balance. If the amounts are the same, perform steps 2–4.

If, however, the amounts aren't identical (and if you're reconciling the account for the first time), still carry out steps 2–4, but also see the Handy Tip on page 186.

Transferring statement data
Carry out the following steps:

1 Click here; select an appropriate account

2 Insert your statement's ending balance

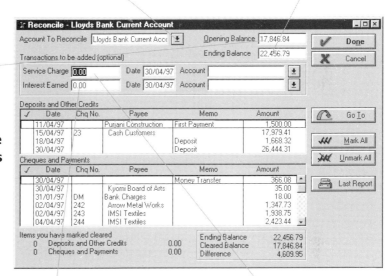

3 Insert any statement interest charges

4 Insert any statement service charges

Now carry out the procedures on the following page.

Now carry out the procedures on the following page.

...contd

Now do the following:

You should perform step 1 for:
- **the Deposits and Other Credits section**
- **the Cheques and Payments section**

Clearing transactions

In the next stage in the reconciliation process, you compare transactions which have been processed by your bank with their equivalents in your account. If they're both present *and* identical (the normal state of affairs), you mark them as 'cleared'.

Follow one of the procedures listed on page 182 to launch the Reconcile dialog. Carry out steps 1–4 (as appropriate) on page 183. Now do the following:

Only follow step 2 if all the transactions in the 'Deposits and Other Credits' and 'Cheques and Payments' sections **match your statement, and if the Difference field (see the Handy Tip on page 185) shows** 0.00.

If the Difference field doesn't show 0.00, **however, omit step 2; instead, carry out the appropriate procedures on the following page.**

1   Click the matched transaction; a ✔ appears against it

2   Click here (but see the Handy Tip on the left)

...contd

If the Difference field (see the Handy Tip) doesn't display 0.00, do the following.

Correcting an existing transaction

Carry out the following steps in the Reconcile dialog:

Repeat steps 1–2 under both headings as often as necessary. When the following is true:

Ending Balance	22,456.79
Cleared Balance	22,456.79
Difference	0.00

This field shows 0.00

reconciliation is complete. Follow step 2 on page 184. If, however, you've carried out the procedures listed here and the Difference field still doesn't show 0.00, follow the further procedures on page 186.

Select a divergent transaction

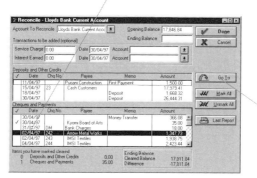

2 Click here

The original transaction window launches. Make the necessary amendments and click OK.

Inserting a missing transaction

Within the Reconcile dialog, press Ctrl+R. Do the following:

Type in the missing transaction

Date	Number	Payee	Account	Payment	✓	Deposit	Balance
30/04/97	DM	Bank Charges	-split-	18.00	✓		7,703.04
30/04/97	258	NPR Property Management	-split-	2,585.00			5,118.04
30/04/97	259	Prichard Chemical & Pain	Accounts Payable	3,965.63			1,152.41
30/04/97			Lloyds Visa	366.08			786.33
05/05/97	20121	Jose Alves	-split-	519.62			266.71
19/05/97	260	Inland Revenue	-split-	466.09			-199.38
28/05/97	261	Brentford Equipment	Accounts Payable	7,575.82			-7,775.20
19/06/97	262	Inland Revenue	-split-	126.13			-7,901.33

Ending balance   -7,901.33

2 Click here; then press Esc to close the register

If you're reconciling an account for the first time, you'll have problems if the Opening Balance you inserted was incorrect (e.g. because there were outstanding transactions). Use the techniques on page 185 to make the necessary amendments now; the Opening Balance field is updated.

   Or pass the relevant internal adjustment.

If, after the procedures on page 185, the Difference field in the Reconcile dialog does not show 0.00, this means there is a discrepancy. Do *one* of the following:

Making an internal adjustment

If the amount of the discrepancy is small, you can write it off. Carry out step 2 on page 184. Then do the following:

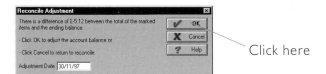

Click here

QuickBooks makes the appropriate internal adjustment, and reconciliation is complete.

Tracking down the discrepancy

It's possible you made one or more errors during the clearing stage. If so, you can try to locate them now. Refer to your statement and count:

•   the number of deposits

•   the number of cheques/withdrawals

Compare these totals with the following section of the Reconcile dialog:

If you can't find the error, your bank may be at fault. If so, inform it and pass an internal adjustment.

   When you next reconcile the account, delete the cleared QuickBooks balancing transaction.

The number of deposits

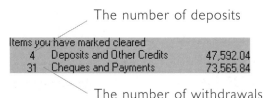

The number of withdrawals

If the number of deposits or withdrawals isn't the same, you'll have a good idea of the *type* of transaction in which the error is located.

When you find the error(s), use the techniques on page 185 to correct them. Then perform step 2 on page 184 to complete reconciliation.

Index

Keyboard shortcuts

Ctrl+A	Launches the Chart of Accounts
Ctrl+J	Launches the Customer:Job list
Ctrl+T	Launches the Memorised Transaction list
Ctrl+I	Launches the Create Invoices window
Ctrl+W	Launches the Write Cheques window
Ctrl+Q	Invokes a QuickReport
Ctrl+Z	Undoes typing
Ctrl+N	(Within a form) Launches a new form
Ctrl+D	Deletes a selected item or transaction
Ctrl+H	Launches the Transaction History window
Ctrl+E	(Within a register) Launches the associated form
	(Within the Chart of Accounts) Edits details of the highlighted account
Ctrl+R	(Within the Chart of Accounts) Launches the highlighted account's register